How Wooden Ships
Are Built

How Wooden Ships Are Built

A Practical Treatise on
Modern American Wooden
Ship Construction with a
Supplement on Laying
Off Wooden Vessels

By H. COLE ESTEP
Editor of The Marine Review

W. W. NORTON & COMPANY

NEW YORK   LONDON

Reprint of the original edition
published in 1918 by The Penton Publishing Company,
Cleveland, Ohio, under the same title

Reprinted by arrangement of
T & A Foxe Ltd, Brattleboro, Vermont

Published simultaneously in Canada by
George J. McLeod Limited, Toronto
Printed in the United States of America
Manufactured by The Murray Printing Company

Library of Congress Cataloging in Publication Data
Estep, H. Cole (Harvey Cole)
  How wooden ships are built.

  Reprint. Originally published: Cleveland, Ohio:
Penton Pub. Co., 1918.
  Includes index.
  1. Ships, Wooden.   2. Ship-building—United States—
History.   I. Title.
VM144.E7   1983   623.8'207   83–42660

ISBN 0-393-03288-4

W. W. Norton & Company, Inc.
500 Fifth Avenue, New York, N.Y. 10110
W. W. Norton & Company Ltd.
37 Great Russell Street, London WC1B 3NU

1 2 3 4 5 6 7 8 9 0

Preface

THE revival of wooden shipbuilding in the United States dates from the latter part of 1915. In April, 1917, at the time we declared war against Germany, over 150 large wooden vessels were under construction along our coasts, principally in New England, the South and the Pacific Northwest. With America's entry into the war, the tonnage requirements of the entente allies were tremendously increased. It soon became evident that the United States would be called upon to construct an enormous armada of steel cargo carriers and in addition as many wooden vessels as could possibly be turned out. Subsequent events up to the spring of 1918 have served only to emphasize the problem. The universal cry is ships, ships—and yet more ships! The necessity, under these conditions, for a large fleet of wooden vessels is no longer disputed, and wooden shipbuilding flourishes all around our far-flung coast line from Maine to Washington.

This revival of the art of wooden shipbuilding has brought with it an insistent demand for information on how wooden ships are built. Compared with the needs of today, the number of expert wooden shipbuilders in the United States at the outbreak of our war with Germany constituted scarcely more than a corporal's guard. Thousands of new men have been inducted into the business. These men must be trained. They must be taught the "know how".

It is to assist in this important work of training that this book is offered. In other words, the book has been prepared to meet a war emergency and it is hoped the information it contains is of practical value.

Most of the material appeared originally in a series of articles published in THE MARINE REVIEW between June, 1917, and March, 1918. The entire text, however, has been carefully revised and brought down to date.

The illustrations, which the publisher believes form perhaps the most valuable feature of the volume, have been carefully selected. Over 150 of the original photographs were made personally by the author expressly for this work. They were taken with the sole purpose of showing clearly and accurately how modern wooden ships actually are constructed. The aim in every case was to present important details of construction rather than general views. To obtain the photographs and collect the material for this work the author traveled extensively and visited nearly all of the important wooden shipyards in the United States.

An effort has been made to produce a book that is practical and illustrative and one that also reflects current American practice accurately.

The mathematical theory of ship design and other details which come more within the province of the naval architect than the shipbuilder have been omitted. As a supplement, however, two chapters on laying down wooden ships from the treatise of the late Samuel J. P. Thearle have been added. Acknowledgment is made to John W. Perrin, librarian, Case Library, Cleveland, for the opportunity to reprint portions of this rare work published originally by William Collins Sons & Co., London. While Professor Thearle deals with laying down British ships of the line, the underlying principles of which he treats are unchangeable and it is doubtful if any present-day author could present the subject more lucidly.

The publisher and author wish to express their appreciation of the generous assistance they received from the leading wooden shipbuilders of the country, without whose aid this work would have been impossible. By permitting full access to their plants and by whole-hearted co-operation in furnishing valuable data, detailed drawings, etc., they have set an example of patriotism and broadmindedness that many lines of business could emulate.

For particular services, advice and assistance the author wishes specially to acknowledge his indebtedness to Capt. James Griffiths and Stanley A. Griffiths, Winslow Marine Railway & Shipbuilding Co., Seattle; S. H. Hedges, Washington Shipping Corp., Seattle; M. R. Ward, Grays Harbor Shipbuilding Co., Aberdeen, Wash.; F. A. Ballin, Supple-Ballin Shipbuilding Corp., Portland, Oreg.; O. P. M. Goss, West Coast Lumberman's association, Seattle; Frank M. Stetson, Stetson Machine Works, Seattle; Martin C. Erismann, naval architect, Houston, Texas; R. Lawrence Smith, New York, and G. W. Hinckley, Brunswick Marine Construction Co., Brunswick, Ga.

Contents

Chapter I — *Typical Methods of Construction*... 1

Chapter II — *Strength and Characteristics of Ship Timbers*............................. 7

Chapter III — *Layout and Equipment of Wooden Shipbuilding Plants*.................. 15

Chapter IV — *Details of Different Types of Wooden Vessels*........................... 23

Chapter V — *Details of Frame and Keel Construction*................................ 33

Chapter VI — *Methods of Framing Forward End of Ship*.............................. 47

Chapter VII — *Framing the After End of the Ship*.................................. 54

Chapter VIII — *Planking, Keelson and Ceiling Construction*.......................... 64

Chapter IX — *Construction of Hold Bracing and Deck Elements*...................... 73

Chapter X — *Spars, Rudders, Shaft Logs and Engine Beds*........................... 83

Supplement

Chapter I — *Fundamental Propositions*.. 87

Chapter II — *Fairing the Lines*... 92

LIST OF ILLUSTRATIONS

PAGE

Fig. 1—Launching a large wooden steamer at a shipyard near New Orleans.. 1

Fig. 2—Detail of keel construction of English ship... 2

Fig. 3—Midship section of a typical nineteenth century English ship 2

Fig. 4—Midship section of a wooden ship designed by a modern Pacific Coast Naval Architect.................... 3

Fig. 5—Midship section of a modern American wooden ship of the conventional type........................ 3

Fig. 6—Typical construction views in a southern wooden shipbuilding yard 4

Fig. 7—Cross section showing method of reinforcement patented by Frank E. Kirby.................... 5

Fig. 8—Fashioning curved and irregular timbers on a band saw 7

Fig. 9—Special machines have been designed for beveling and edging timbers 7

Fig. 10—Timbers long enough to require two cars frequently are needed in wooden shipbuilding.................. 8

Fig. 11—Boring holes with an air drill.. 8

Fig. 12—Typical lumbering scenes in the northwest.. 11

Fig. 13—West Coast lumbering requires special heavy duty equipment 12

Fig. 14—Division of stringer into volumes for consideration of positions of knots 13

Fig. 15—A well laid out wooden shipyard located in the center of a large city.................... 14

Fig. 16—Electrically-driven traveling derrick setting frames in a wooden shipyard................ 15

Fig. 17—Wooden shipyard located on naturally sloping ground with an abundance of room.................. 16

Fig. 18—A small yard laid out on long narrow strip of ground 16

Fig. 19—Yard laid out on irregular plot of ground.. 16

Fig. 20—Yard with four building slips compactly arranged on city property 17

Fig. 21—A steel framed revolving crane for wooden shipyard 17

Fig. 22—Mill containing saws and woodworking machinery.. 18

Fig. 23—Cut-off and band saw sheds in a western shipyard.. 18

Fig. 24—General view of a Seattle shipyard showing beveling machine, arrangement of derricks, building slips, etc. 19

Fig. 25—Woodworking machinery in a Puget Sound shipyard 20

Fig. 26—Bandsawing bevels in a South Atlantic shipyard.. 20

Fig. 27—Derricks and hoisting engine in a southern yard.. 20

Fig. 28—Timber hauling engines in a Grays Harbor shipyard 20

Fig. 29—Driving piles for building ways in a Georgia shipyard 20

Fig. 30—General arrangement of building ways showing vessels in various stages of construction.................. 21

Fig. 31—Portable electrically driven planer.. 21

Fig. 32—Band sawing equipment in a Pacific Coast yard.. 21

Fig. 33—Traveling table for handling timber around machines 21

Fig. 34—A building shed protects the work from the weather 21

Fig. 35—A 5-masted, topmast wooden auxiliary schooner built at a prominent Pacific Coast shipyard............. 23

Fig. 36—Midship section and construction details of a 290-foot, 5-masted topmast auxiliary schooner............. 24

Fig. 37—Midship section and construction details of 4000-ton wooden steamer designed for construction on the Pacific coast 25

Fig. 38—A 5-masted wooden auxiliary schooner undergoing her trial trip........................ 26

Fig. 39—Three-thousand-ton, 4-masted schooner built at Seattle, Wash.......................... 26

Fig. 40—Midship section and construction details of a 4000-ton motor ship with diagonal planking............. 27

Fig. 41—Outboard profile and deck plan of a typical 4000-ton wooden steamship 28

Fig. 42—Outboard profile and deck plan of 4500-ton wooden steamship with propelling machinery aft............ 28

Fig. 43—Outboard profile and deck plan of 4000-ton motor ship designed for overseas service.................. 29

Fig. 44—Inboard profile of 5-masted, topmast auxiliary schooner showing arrangement of center girder-keelson... 30

Fig. 45—A typical 4-masted wooden auxiliary schooner under construction on Puget Sound........................ 31

Fig. 46—Frame of a typical wooden vessel nearly ready for planking 33

Fig. 47—Laying-down the lines of a ship on the mold-loft floor 34

Fig. 48—Laying the keel of a 4000-ton motor ship.. 34

Fig. 49—Finishing the framing of a large wooden ship on the Pacific coast 34

LIST OF ILLUSTRATIONS

PAGE

FIG. 50—FRAMING STAGE LAID ALONGSIDE KEEL—THE FRAMES ARE HOISTED INTO POSITION BY MEANS OF A SIMPLE TACKLE...... 35
FIG. 51—ASSEMBLING FRAME FUTTOCKS ON FRAMING STAGE.. 35
FIG. 52—RESAWING FRAME JOINTS TO A PROPER FIT.. 35
FIG. 53—SETTING KEEL BLOCKS TO THE PROPER HEIGHT.. 36
FIG. 54—SETTING KEEL BLOCKS ON SAND.. 36
FIG. 55—KEEL WEDGED IN PLACE ON KEEL BLOCKS.. 36
FIG. 56—LAYING THE KEEL IN A SOUTHERN SHIPYARD.. 36
FIG. 57—SCAFFOLDING ARRANGED ALONGSIDE KEEL BLOCKS.. 36
FIG. 58—KEEL NEAR STERN 36
FIG. 59—FRAME TIMBERS AND MOLDS 37
FIG. 60—MARKING FRAME TIMBERS 37
FIG. 61—CUT-OFF SAW FOR FRAME TIMBERS.. 37
FIG. 62—BAND SAW FOR SHAPING FRAME TIMBERS.. 37
FIG. 63—A FRAME BUTTOCK AFTER LEAVING THE BAND SAW.. 37
FIG. 64—GENERAL ARRANGEMENT OF FRAMING STAGE... 37
FIG. 65—SETTING FRAMES BY MEANS OF A TRAVELING CRANE... 38
FIG. 66—RAISING FRAMES BY MEANS OF BLOCK AND TACKLE... 38
FIG. 67—FRAMES RAISED, READY FOR PLUMBING AND HORNING... 38
FIG. 68—HAND-WINCH FOR HAULING TIMBERS THROUGH BAND SAW... 39
FIG. 69—DETAIL OF BOLTED FRAME JOINTS 39
FIG. 70—ANOTHER VIEW OF BOLTED FRAME CONSTRUCTION... 39
FIG. 71—RIBBANDS IN PLACE AND SHORING UNDER FRAME.. 39
FIG. 72—FRAMING STAGE IN A GEORGIA SHIPYARD.. 40
FIG. 73—FRAME OF A VESSEL IN A GEORGIA SHIPYARD... 40
FIG. 74—TWO SETS OF CROSS SPALLS SOMETIMES ARE USED TO HOLD THE FRAME SECTIONS TOGETHER.............. 40
FIG. 75—UPPER PART OF ARCH STRAPPING... 41
FIG. 76—LOWER PART OF ARCH STRAPPING SHOWING METHOD OF FASTENING THE BUTTS.......................... 41
FIG. 77—DETAIL OF STANDARD FRAME CONSTRUCTION... 42
FIG. 78—DETAIL OF BOLTED FRAME CONSTRUCTION... 42
FIG. 79—FRAME NEAR BOW USING NATURAL CROOKS.. 42
FIG. 80—FRAMING A SHIP IN A SOUTHERN YARD.. 42
FIG. 81—SOMETIMES THE FLOORS ARE LAID FIRST AND THE FRAME PIECES RAISED AFTERWARD..................... 42
FIG. 82—DETAIL OF FRAMES HEELING TO DEADWOOD.. 42
FIG. 83—BOW CONSTRUCTION OF A LARGE PACIFIC COAST MOTOR SCHOONER 46
FIG. 84—DETAILS OF STEM SHOWING LARGE NATURAL KNEE.. 47
FIG. 85—STEM REINFORCED WITHOUT USE OF A KNEE.. 48
FIG. 86—DETAILED DRAWING OF STEM OF A STEAMER THE GENERAL ARRANGEMENT OF WHICH IS SHOWN IN FIG. 84.......... 48
FIG. 87—INTERIOR OF BOW CONSTRUCTION OF A 290-FOOT MOTOR SCHOONER 49
FIG. 88—DETAIL OF STEM CONSTRUCTION OF THE SCHOONER SHOWN IN FIG. 87 ILLUSTRATING METHOD OF FASTENING FORWARD
    ENDS OF KEELSON TIMBERS TO STEM.. 49
FIG. 89—ARRANGEMENT OF STEM AND KNIGHTHEAD AT UPPER END NEAR MAIN DECK............................... 49
FIG. 90—STAGING SURROUNDING A CLIPPER-TYPE BOW UNDER CONSTRUCTION 49
FIG. 91—DETAILS OF FOREFOOT SHOWING USE OF NATURAL KNEE AND ANGLE BLOCKS 51
FIG. 92—ANOTHER VIEW OF THE SAME STEM... 51
FIG. 93—SAME STEM FROM THE OPPOSITE SIDE... 51
FIG. 94—STEAMER TYPE BOW UNDER CONSTRUCTION PARTLY PLANKED 51
FIG. 95—STEAMER TYPE BOW FINISHED WITH STAGING STILL IN PLACE 51
FIG. 96—FORWARD CANT FRAMES HEELING TO DEADWOOD.. 51
FIG. 97—DETAIL OF FOREFOOT OF CLIPPER TYPE STEM SHOWING NATURAL KNEE LOCK-SCARFED TO KEEL............. 52
FIG. 98—ARRANGEMENT OF FLOORS, KEELSON AND STEM OF A VESSEL UNDER CONSTRUCTION AT A GULF SHIPYARD.......... 52
FIG. 99—DETAILS OF STEM AND FORWARD FRAME CONSTRUCTION OF A MOTOR SCHOONER UNDER CONSTRUCTION ON THE GULF.... 52
FIG. 100—DETAIL OF STERN FRAME OF SHIP BEING BUILT FOR UNITED STATES GOVERNMENT 54
FIG. 101—FINISHED TRANSOM STERN ON A 5-MASTED MOTOR SCHOONER 54
FIG. 102—DETAIL OF RUDDER AND RUDDERPOST ASSEMBLY.. 54
FIG. 103—DETAIL OF UPPER PART OF STERN FRAMING SHOWN IN FIG. 102 55
FIG. 104—GENERAL VIEW OF STERN FRAMES AND RUDDER ASSEMBLY 55
FIG. 105—ERECTING FORE AND AFT POST TIMBERS FOR A STERN OF UNUSUALLY STRONG CONSTRUCTION 55
FIG. 106—DETAIL OF TRANSOM STERN FRAMING OF A SHIP UNDER CONSTRUCTION IN A SOUTHERN YARD.............. 56

PAGE

FIG. 107—TRANSOM TYPE STERN IN EARLY STAGES OF CONSTRUCTION 56

FIG. 108—THE NEXT STEP IN THE CONSTRUCTION OF A TRANSOM STERN 56

FIG. 109—INTERIOR OF A TRANSOM STERN BEFORE TRANSOM TIMBERS ARE IN PLACE 56

FIG. 110—A CLOSER VIEW OF THE INTERIOR OF THE SAME STERN................................ 56

FIG. 111—FITTING TRANSOM TIMBERS TO FASHION TIMBER................................ 56

FIG. 112—STERN FRAME ASSEMBLY BEING HOISTED INTO PLACE................................ 57

FIG. 113—DETAIL OF FRAMING OF TRANSOM TYPE STERN................................ 57

FIG. 114—INSIDE OF FRAMING OF THE STERN SHOWN IN FIG. 113................................ 57

FIG. 115—DETAIL OF STERN FRAMING FROM THE INSIDE OF A SHIP................................ 58

FIG. 116—ANOTHER VIEW OF THE FRAMING OF THE SAME SHIP................................ 58

FIG. 117—LOWER PART OF STERN FRAMING OF THE SAME SHIP SHOWING STERNPOST, DEADWOOD, ETC........................ 58

FIG. 118—SAME STERN PLANKED UP AND NEARLY FINISHED................................ 58

FIG. 119—DETAILS OF THE ELLIPTICAL OR FANTAIL STERN SHOWN IN FIGS. 105 AND 125................................ 59

FIG. 120—TIMBER FROM WHICH QUARTER-BLOCK IS HEWED................................ 60

FIG. 121—HEWING OUT THE QUARTER-BLOCK................................ 60

FIG. 122—A PAIR OF QUARTER-BLOCKS FINISHED................................ 60

FIG. 123—STERN FRAMING SHOWING HOLES LEFT FOR RECEPTION OF QUARTER-BLOCKS 60

FIG. 124—QUARTER-BLOCK IN PLACE 60

FIG. 125—GENERAL VIEW OF ELLIPTICAL OR FANTAIL STERN................................ 60

FIG. 126—ANOTHER VIEW OF THE STERN SHOWN IN FIG. 125................................ 61

FIG. 127—NATURAL KNEE USED TO CONNECT STERNPOST TO OTHER STERN ELEMENTS 61

FIG. 128—SHAFT LOG IN TWIN-SCREW MOTOR SHIP................................ 61

FIG. 129—DETAIL OF FANTAIL STERN CONSTRUCTION AT KNUCKLE LINE 62

FIG. 130—ARRANGEMENT OF TIMBERS INSIDE THE SAME STERN AT THE POINT SHOWN IN FIG. 129........................ 62

FIG. 131—TIMBER CHUTE FOR HAULING CEILING STRAKES AND KEELSONS INSIDE THE SHIP........................ 64

FIG. 132—INTERIOR OF A WOODEN SHIP UNDER CONSTRUCTION SHOWING TIMBER CHUTE AND SCAFFOLDING—BILGE CEILING IN
        PLACE 64

FIG. 133—STEAM BOX FOR SOFTENING PLANKS................................ 65

FIG. 134—SIDE OF SHIP WITH PLANK IN PLACE................................ 65

FIG. 135—DUBBING-OFF AND RAISING LINES ON SHIP'S SIDE FOR PLANKING 65

FIG. 136—CLAMPING PLANK IN PLACE PRIOR TO SPIKING................................ 65

FIG. 137—CLAMPING CEILING STRAKES IN PLACE PRIOR TO BOLTING................................ 65

FIG. 138—LOWER ENDS OF STERN FRAME AND DEADWOOD RASED FOR PLANKING 66

FIG. 139—CEILING A SHIP IN A GULF COAST YARD................................ 66

FIG. 140—BOLTING DOWN KEELSON TIMBERS WITH PNEUMATIC HAMMERS 66

FIG. 141—PORT SIDE OF A COMPLETELY CEILED WOODEN MOTOR SHIP................................ 67

FIG. 142—BEVELING KEELSON TIMBERS BY HAND................................ 68

FIG. 143—MAKING A SCARF IN A KEELSON TIMBER................................ 68

FIG. 144—THE FIRST STEP IN BUILDING UP A CENTER GIRDER-KEELSON 68

FIG. 145—CLAMPS USED FOR TEMPORARILY SECURING KEELSON PIECES 68

FIG. 146—BORING DRIFTBOLT HOLES IN CENTER GIRDER-KEELSON................................ 68

FIG. 147—CENTER GIRDER-KEELSON NEARLY COMPLETED................................ 68

FIG. 148—CEILING STRAKES ON A TABLE OF AUTOMATIC BEVELING MACHINE—NOTE BATTEN ALONG TOP WHICH INDICATES THE
        AMOUNT OF BEVEL 69

FIG. 149—IN SOME YARDS THE CEILING IS LAID IN PARALLEL STRAKES BETWEEN THE KEELSONS AND THE BILGE.............. 69

FIG. 150—DUBBING-OFF THE INSIDE PREPARATORY TO CEILING................................ 69

FIG. 151—KEELSON CONSTRUCTION OF A SMALL MOTOR SCHOONER................................ 69

FIG. 152—CLAMPING AND BOLTING UPPER CEILING STRAKES IN PLACE 70

FIG. 153—CEILING A SHIP IN THE WAY OF THE STERN, SHOWING THE USE OF CLAMPS................................ 70

FIG. 154—DETAIL OF STANCHION FOOTINGS IN A LARGE WOODEN SHIP 73

FIG. 155—GENERAL VIEW OF STANCHIONS IN THE SAME SHIP................................ 73

FIG. 156—STANCHIONS BETWEEN MAIN AND LOWER DECK BEAMS................................ 74

FIG. 157—GENERAL VIEW OF HOLD FRAMING................................ 74

FIG. 158—SAFETY LADDER INSIDE SHIP................................ 74

FIG. 159—DUBBING-OFF STERN BULWARKS................................ 74

FIG. 160—ARRANGEMENT OF DECK BEAMS NEAR STERN................................ 75

FIG. 161—DECK OF WOODEN MOTOR SCHOONER NEARLY COMPLETED................................ 75

FIG. 162—DECK BEAMS RESTING ON SHELF, BOLTED CONSTRUCTION................................ 75

PAGE

Fig. 163—Details of fastenings of shelf and clamp... 75

Fig. 164—Main-deck beams with hanging knees in place... 76

Fig. 165—Main deck beams fitted to shelf... 76

Fig. 166—Spiking down deck planking 76

Fig. 167—Clamping deck planking in place.. 76

Fig. 168—General view of hold beams showing lumber chute 77

Fig. 169—Detail of cast steel knees... 77

Fig. 170—Hold beams in the way of a hatch... 77

Fig. 171—Lodging knees in the way of a hatch.. 77

Fig. 172—Detail of hatch beam construction.. 77

Fig. 173—Crane used for setting deck beams.. 77

Fig. 174—Surfacing knees on a special planing machine—knees also are fayed on this machine in lots of 10 or 12, the operation requiring only 15 minutes.. 78

Fig. 175—Section of deck framing of large wooden ship showing method of reinforcing with steel plates and straps 78

Fig. 176—Deck of large wooden motor schooner... 79

Fig. 177—Caulking deck using heavy maul.. 79

Fig. 178—Finish caulking 79

Fig. 179—Inserting pine plugs over spikeheads in deck... 79

Fig. 180—Rudder details of a 4000-ton wooden vessel... 82

Fig. 181—Foundation details for a twin-screw oil-engine driven ship fitted with 500-horsepower, 6-cylinder engines 83

Fig. 182—Iron-bark rudder stock set up on traveling table of beveling machine 84

Fig. 183—Angle chocks used for trimming rudder stock on beveling machine 84

Fig. 184—Complete iron-bark rudder for wooden ship... 84

Fig. 185—Roughing out a spar with an axe... 85

Fig. 186—Steam-driven cargo winch installed on wooden ship 85

Fig. 187—Finishing a spar with a hand plane.. 85

Fig. 188—Steam-driven anchor winch built on Pacific coast.. 85

Midship section standard wooden steamer for government.. 6

New wooden vessels vie with steel.. 72

Supplement

How Wooden Ships Are Laid Off

PAGE

Fig. 1—Projecting a point on a plane.. 88

Fig. 2—Determining a point in space.. 88

Fig. 3—Rabatting a line.. 88

Fig. 4—Sheer draft of a sloop of war... 88

Fig. 5—Waterlines and diagonals 92

Fig. 6—Diagram showing method of ending level lines.. 93

Fig. 7—Correct method of drawing bearding line... 93

Fig. 8—Diagram showing method of drawing a horizontal ribband line 94

Fig. 9—Buttock lines and bow lines... 94

Fig. 10—Contracted method of fairing... 95

Fig. 11—Accounting for swell for screw shaft... 95

Fig. 12—Diagram showing method of drawing diagonals in sheer plan 97

How Wooden Ships
Are Built

How Wooden Ships Are Built

CHAPTER I

Typical Methods of Construction

WOODEN shipbuilding was a lost art which the gods of war decreed must be revived. When the European war broke out in 1914, there were over forty-six and a half million tons of merchant steamers afloat. Most of them were steel cargo vessels suitable for overseas trade. As nearly as can be estimated, the submarines accounted for nearly one-fifth of this tonnage up to Jan. 1, 1918. A tremendous revival of shipbuilding the world over has been the natural reaction to this situation.

Soon after the United States declared war it became evident that it would be necessary to construct a large fleet of wooden vessels to supplement the enormous tonnage of steel ships which the emergencies of war demanded. Although the original chimera of a fleet of a thousand or more wooden cargo carriers loosed on the seas to bear the brunt of the submarine attack has properly faded from the public mind, the wooden ship remains an exceedingly tangible factor in our shipbuilding program. At the end of 1917 the United States Emergency Fleet corporation had let contracts for 379 wooden steamships with an aggregate deadweight tonnage of 1,344,900. In addition 58 composite vessels had been contracted for with an aggregate tonnage of 207,000. If properly constructed, these vessels may be used

for transatlantic service. At all events they will be suitable for many coastwise purposes, thus releasing valuable steel steamers for work overseas.

The wooden ship is a necessity in the present emergency. The ranks of "the little cargo boats that sail the wet seas roun'" have been seriously thinned by the unholy submarine warfare of the German empire. The dingy tramps of the ocean lanes, England's and America's pride, are threatened, and unlike the situation described by Kipling in 1894, the man-o'-war has found himself unable "to up an' fight for them" with complete success, although tremendous forward strides in the offensive against the submarines were made during 1917.

In the meantime, while a method of completely exterminating the German pest is being evolved, and long after the last one has been swept from the seas, shipbuilders everywhere will be obliged to proceed at top speed to provide vessels sorely needed by the

world's commerce. When trade revives after the war, the demands for tonnage will be so great that it now appears both wooden and steel shipbuilders are assured a long period of prosperity and profitable activity.

All sensible men recognize the merits of the steel ship. Its superior effectiveness in many directions is readily acknowledged. But we are now face to face with a great national emergency in meeting which the wooden vessel has a definite function to perform.

Therefore, mallets and saws are busy throughout the great length of our seaboard from Maine to Texas and from California to Washington building a host of wooden vessels. As a result of this activity there has grown up a demand for information of a practical character on wooden shipbuilding which it is the purpose of this book to supply.

How large may wooden vessels be built? This is one of the first questions that arises in considering the construction of wooden cargo carriers, for the economies of large units are thoroughly appreciated throughout the maritime world. In the heydey of the wooden ship, in England and Europe about 1850, very few vessels larger than 2000 tons were constructed, and practically none were over 40 feet beam. Their length was usually about 200 feet. Their tonnage was limited by the fact that the

FIG. 1—LAUNCHING A LARGE WOODEN STEAMER AT A SHIPYARD NEAR NEW ORLEANS

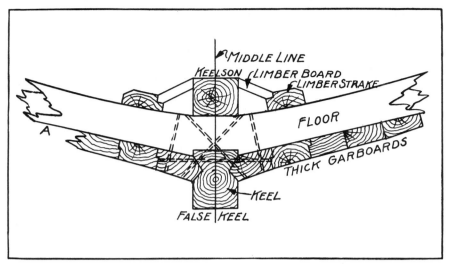

FIG. 2—DETAIL OF KEEL CONSTRUCTION OF ENGLISH SHIP

naturally crooked oak timbers used for the frames grew only in limited sizes. The same limitations existed in regard to long timbers, such as keels, keelsons, strakes, clamps, shelves and planks, which had to be built up and well scarfed, locked, hooked and bolted to make up for lack of large size material. It remained for the Pacific coast of the United States with its boundless supply of timbers of the largest sizes, to finally demonstrate that wooden vessels of 3000 to 3500 or oven 4000 tons deadweight capacity are practicable. There is, however, a difference of opinion among architects as to the extent to which the largest hulls should be reinforced with steel. In 1917, two wooden vessels, 308 feet long, 285 feet keel, with a deadweight capacity of 4300 tons, not including 2500 barrels of oil fuel for diesel engines, were built on the north Pacific coast. These vessels, which are so reinforced with steel as to fall almost in the composite classification, have been given the highest rating by both American and British classification societies. Conservative opinion leans to the view that vessels without steel reinforcement should not be built over 260 or 270 feet in length. For any vessel over 200 feet arch strapping, at least, seems desirable.

As far as the supply of lumber for wooden ship construction is concerned, there is little to fear. The estimated total supply of merchantable timber in the United States is placed at the stupendous figure 2,500,000,000,000 feet board measure—over two-thousand billion feet. Canada, in addition has 80,000,000,000 feet. Russia has even more timber reserves than the United States. A large portion of the shipbuilding timber in this country is in the Pacific northwest, the state of Washington alone having over 11,700 square miles of standing timber, exclusive of national forest reserves. In the south, along the gulf and southern Atlantic coasts, there are almost equally important timber reserves, and on account of its superior strength, southern pine is prized for shipbuilding, although it does not grow as large as western fir. Also, in spite of 300 years of exploitation, the forests of New England still contain vast quantities of ship timber of unusually satisfactory character.

In fact, New England is one of the two sections of the country in which wooden ship building maintained a continuous existence through the lean years, 1880 to 1916. The north Pacific coast is the only other region where the art of building wooden vessels failed of complete extinction during the period just mentioned. It is from the traditions of both of these important sections, separated by 3,000 miles of continent, that the revived art and the new literature of wooden ship building must be drawn.

Power for Wooden Ships

Wooden hulls are best adapted to sail power, but for obvious reasons such a method of propulsion cannot be depended upon in modern times, except for certain special trades. In the war zones, sailing ships are under a severe handicap because of their high visibility. Some form of mechanical propulsion, therefore, is desirable for practically all of the wooden vessels now under construction or to be built during the next 24 months. Virtually only three types of power present themselves, oil engines of the

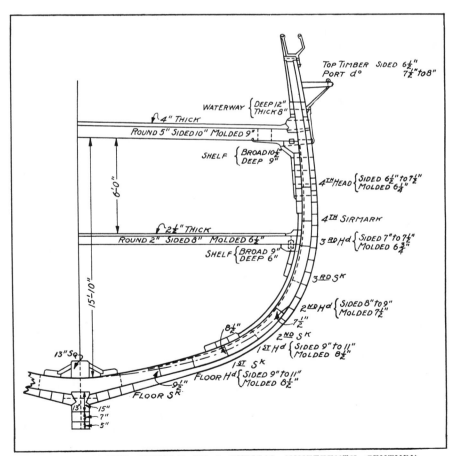

FIG. 3—MIDSHIP SECTION OF A TYPICAL NINETEENTH CENTURY
ENGLISH SHIP

pure or semi-diesel type, reciprocating steam engines and steam turbines.

The advantages of the oil engine in fuel economy, increased cargo space, low visibility, etc., are well known, and for these reasons a large number of the wooden vessels built in 1916-17 were fitted with internal combustion motors, usually working twin screws. Undoubtedly, this arrangement is one of the most satisfactory that could be devised for large wooden merchant ships. But it has been shown there are not enough skilled oil engine builders in the country to supply the demand at the present time. Therefore recourse is had to steam. The question of obtaining enough skilled engineers also enters into this problem.

For a full-powered ship, the concensus of opinion seems to be that about 1,500 horsepower is necessary for propelling a 3,000-ton vessel. In spite of the advantages of the oil engine, steam is not without its advocates, especially among those who point out the space saving possibilities of the turbine.

Types of Hull Construction

Compared with steel vessels, wooden ships are weak in both longitudinal and transverse directions, although their greatest structural failings appear to be in longitudinal planes. Large wooden hulls are susceptible to both hogging and sagging. In the former case, the deck bends convexly, the ends becoming lower than the midship section; in the case of sagging, the deck bends concavely and the sheer is exaggerated. Also,

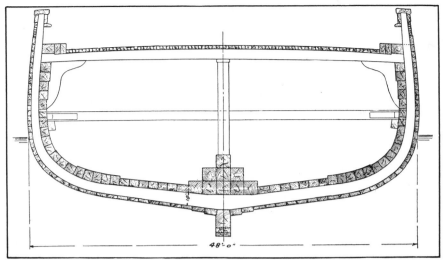

FIG. 5—MIDSHIP SECTION OF A MODERN AMERICAN WOODEN SHIP OF THE CONVENTIONAL TYPE

in a seaway, some wooden hulls are sprung up from the bottom, causing the decks to bulge. These weaknesses are largely due to the rectangular construction of wooden ships, in which the fastenings are depended upon almost exclusively for stiffness.

In the nature of things, it is impossible to fasten the members of a wooden vessel together as stiffly as those of a steel ship, but by proper design and construction a great deal of the weakness inherent in wooden hulls may be overcome. If we consider a ship as a beam and resort to the language of the engineer for a moment, we find that the greatest strength should be concentrated as far from the neutral axis (approximately the center of the load waterline plane) as possible; also, the sides of the vessel should be designed to withstand permanent vertical and longitudinal stresses; and the connections between the flange and web members (decks and sides) should be as rigid as possible.

Typical Wooden Vessels

The accompanying cross sections of typical wooden ships show how designers in various parts of the world and at different times have attempted to meet these conditions.

Fig. 3 shows the cross section of an English sailing ship built to rigid specifications about 1850. This vessel was 30 feet beam and about 180 feet in length. A detail of the keel construction is shown in Fig. 2. This ship had considerably more deadrise than a modern cargo carrier, that is her bottom was much less flat than is now customary, and this rounded construction added tremendously to her strength. In addition, she had two decks, the lower deck beams being 6½ x 8 inches and the main

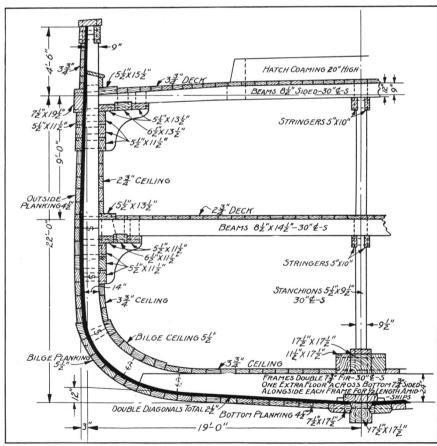

FIG. 4—MIDSHIP SECTION OF A WOODEN SHIP DESIGNED BY A MODERN PACIFIC COAST NAVAL ARCHITECT

FIG. 6—TYPICAL CONSTRUCTION VIEWS IN A SOUTHERN WOODEN SHIPBUILDING YARD

deck beams 9 x 10 inches. Finally, she was very carefully and painstakingly fitted together in order to give the utmost stiffness and permanency to the hull structure.

Fig. 5 shows a cross section of a modern Pacific coast lumber vessel of the conventional type. It forms an interesting comparison with Fig. 3. This ship is 48 feet beam and about 275 feet in length. Her floors are 18 inches deep, compared with 9½ inches in the English ship shown in Fig. 3. But in the latter case, natural bent oak was used for the frames and in the modern Pacific coast boat, sawn fir. Some architects think that the depth of the frames in the vessel shown in Fig. 5 is too small. This illustration, however, shows very clearly the characteristics of customary American construction. The feature of the design is the large number of keelsons, nine in all, running from stem to stern like a small mountain range. Fig. 5 also indicates the large size of the planking and ceiling timbers.

A more advanced form of construction, designed by Fred A. Ballin, naval architect, Portland, Ore., is shown in Fig. 4. In this case the

necessity for a large number of keelsons is obviated, in the designer's opinion, by the use of deep floors

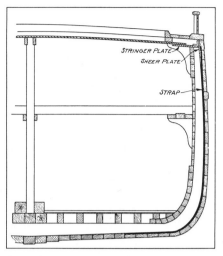

FIG. 7 — CROSS SECTION SHOWING METHOD OF REINFORCEMENT PATENTED BY FRANK E. KIRBY

and deck beams. Care also is taken in the disposal of the knees, ceiling and planking.

One of the most successful forms of steel reinforcement for wood vessels is shown in Fig. 7, illustrating a method of construction patented by Frank E. Kirby, of Detroit, one of the most famous naval architects on the Great Lakes, where a large number of unusually staunch wooden vessels were built in the era before the steel freighter. According to Mr. Kirby's patent, the topsides are strengthened by means of a steel sheer plate, to which a deck stringer plate is connected with a strong angle. The deck stringer rests directly on the top of the top timbers of the frames and the iron straps running diagonally around the hull are fastened to the sheer plate. This is somewhat similar to the method of reinforcement adopted for the new wooden steamers being built for the government under the auspices of the United States Shipping Board Emergency Fleet Corporation, except that in the case of the government boats the deck stringer construction is lighter.

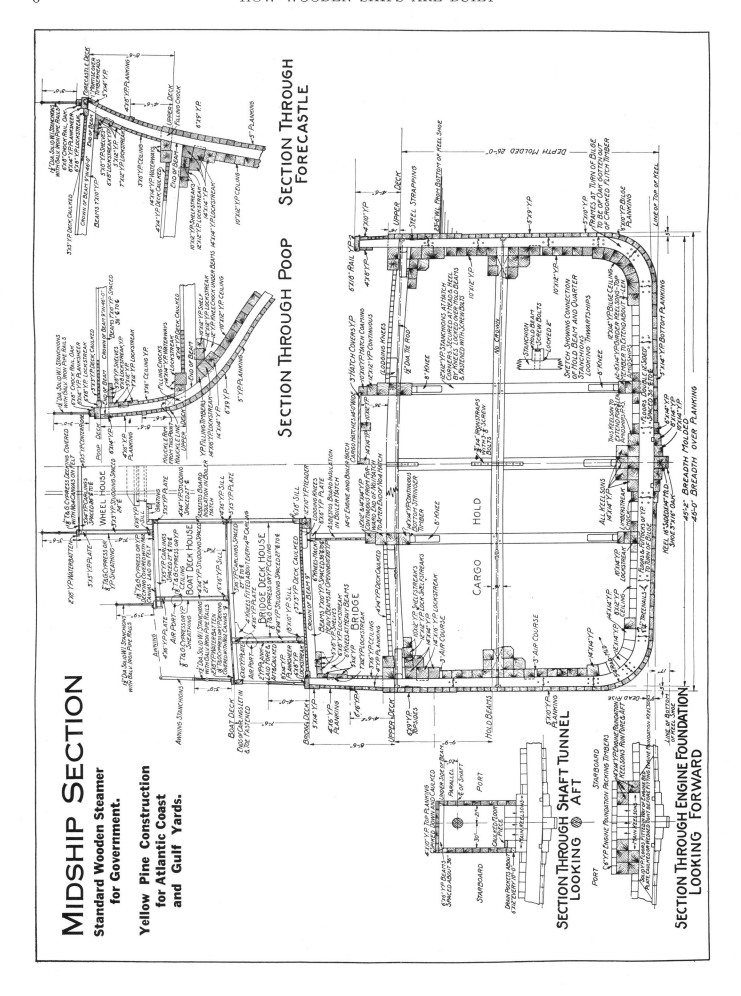

CHAPTER II

Strength and Characteristics of Ship Timbers

BEFORE any attempt is made to lay down or build a wooden ship, the architect, yard superintendent and others responsible for the success of the proposed vessel, should acquire a fundamental knowledge of the physical characteristics and strength of the timbers that will be used in the construction of the hull. An investigation also should be made into the different methods of fastening timbers together in shipbuilding and of the efficiency of such fastenings. In other words, a little knowledge of the elements of structural engineering is as essential to the shipbuilder as it is to the building contractor or bridge erector.

For an intelligent and thorough grasp of the subject it is necessary, in fact, to start with the lumber industry, which bears the same relation to wooden shipbuilding as iron-ore mining does to the manufacture of steel. In this chapter, therefore, a few facts will be presented regarding the production of lumber in the United States, together with data on the physical characteristics and strength of various species of ship timbers.

In the preceding chapter, figures covering the supply of merchantable timber in the United States and Canada were presented. To give an idea of the ability of lumber manufacturers to fur-

nish ship timbers in quantity, it may be stated that the United States forest service has estimated the lumber production of the United States in 1915, the latest year for which figures are available, at 37,013,294,000 board feet. During 1915 there were 29,941 mills in operation. The details of the lumber cut of 1915, showing the number of mills and production of each state are given in Table III. By an inspection of this table, it is possible to estimate the production of the two principal kinds of ship lumber, namely, Douglas fir and southern yellow pine. The pine growing states turned out 17,010,000,000 feet and the fir states, 5,640,000,000 feet in 1915. In 1916, the production of the fir states was approximately 7,000,000,000 feet. About 10 per cent of the Pacific coast cut is available for ship work. In other words, as far as lumber supply is concerned, the Pacific coast mills alone can turn out sufficient material for 400 3000-ton ships in a year and the southern mills, because of the smaller size of pine timbers, enough for 500 to 600 more, provided satisfactory labor supply and mill conditions can be obtained.

Southern yellow pine is the most abundant of all ship materials, and on account of its wide geographical distribution, comparatively close to the great eastern centers of population, it is

extensively employed in building wooden vessel of all kinds. It comes in sufficiently large sizes so that the principal elements of the ship's structure can be worked up in a comparatively few pieces, without the necessity of resorting to an abnormal number of butts and scarfs. Yellow pine is an even grained, easily worked, dense wood Detailed figures on the strength of pine timbers are given in Tables I, II and IV.

Pine is an unusually durable wood, even when subjected to long continued stresses in a ship's structure. In the tables just referred to, the modulus of rupture, or breaking strength, of southern pine is given as varying from 6437 to 5948 pounds per square inch for the green material and 7033 to 5957 pounds for air-seasoned timber. The weight per cubic foot varies from 38.6 to 31.4 pounds. Ships constructed of southern pine along the Atlantic and gulf coasts have a special strength advantage, in that, when possible, natural crooks have been used for the curved frame members in nearly all cases. Such timbers are appreciably stronger than the sawed frame construction. As a material which is suitable for ship construction, Douglas fir, grown on the Pacific coast, is fully as important as yellow pine, and on account of the exceptionally large size of the trees, and the relative light-

FIG. 8—FASHIONING SHIP TIMBERS ON A BAND SAW

FIG. 9—SPECIAL MACHINES HAVE BEEN DESIGNED FOR BEVELING AND EDGING TIMBERS

FIG. 10—TIMBERS LONG ENOUGH TO REQUIRE TWO CARS FREQUENTLY
ARE NEEDED IN WOODEN SHIPBUILDING

ness of the wood, this timber has peculiar advantages of its own. Concerning this wood, the United States forest service, in Bulletin No. 88, has put itself on record as follows:

"Douglas fir may perhaps be considered the most important of American woods. Though in point of production it ranks second to southern yellow pine, its rapid growth in the Pacific coast forests, its comparatively wide distribution and the great variety of uses to which its wood may be put, place it first. As a structural timber it is not surpassed and probably it is most widely used and known in this capacity."

Fir an Important Wood

Douglas fir comprises more than 25 per cent of the standing timber supply of the United States, including both hard and soft woods. The timber stand of Washington and Oregon is such as to insure a permanent source of supply of the highest class of lumber for shipbuilding. Also, the winter climate in this vast, western timber-belt is mild, enabling the lumber camps and mills to operate continuously, thereby producing a steady supply of manufactured products.

Practically all log transportation is by water and many of the mills are located on tidewater, in close proximity to shipbuilding plants. These conditions make it possible to produce lumber for ship construction at a minimum operating cost.

Pacific coast logging operators are provided with equipment specially adapted for handling large logs. Under the ordinary methods of procedure, the logs are hauled out from the places where the trees are felled by steel cables operated by powerful hoisting engines. This operation is termed yarding. The yarded logs are usually rolled onto flat cars or specially constructed trucks, on which they are hauled to the water, either a river or tidewater. Here they are made up into rafts and towed to the mills. To some mills, of course, the logs are delivered direct by rail.

Big Timbers are Cut

The mills on the Pacific coast are equipped with extra heavy facilities for handling big logs and getting out big timbers and heavy planks specially suited to ship construction. Both large circular and band saws are used to work up the logs, while heavy planing mills are provided to dress the timbers. The modern mills are also completely provided with power-driven roller tables and transfers for handling the lumber during the process of manufacture. The accompanying illustrations show the essentials of the logging and lumbering operations on the Pacific coast.

Douglas fir trees grow commonly from 3 to 5 feet in diameter and from 175 to 250 feet high. Tremendous timbers, particularly suited to shipbuilding, therefore are available in quantity. Structural timbers of Douglas fir, 18 x 18 inches in section and 120 to 140 feet long, may be obtained from mills at any time, and timbers 36 inches square and 80 or 90 feet long are equally available. By the use of such timbers, the largest boats can be constructed with a minimum of splicing and scarfing, which not only reduces labor costs but materially increases the strength or seaworthiness of the vessel.

Douglas fir has an average specific gravity of 0.53 based on its oven dry volume. The specific gravity based on green volume, before shrinkage, is 0.46; based on air-dry volume it is 0.48. The green wood weighs 38 pounds per cubic foot, or 3.166 pounds per board foot and the air-dry wood 34 pounds per cubic foot or 2.836 pounds per board foot. These weights vary in fir as in other woods but the foregoing figures are reliable averages. A knowledge of these figures is indispensable to the naval architect or shipbuilder, in computing the weights, trim and displacement of his vessel. The method of figuring these weights will be brought out later in this book. Too many wooden ships at the present time are constructed and trimmed by guesswork, resulting in some exceedingly costly experiences for the shipowner.

Preservatives are Recommended

Douglas fir and southern pine are on a par as to durability, although like other woods when used for shipbuilding, precautions should be taken at the time the boat is constructed to see that preservatives are effectively applied and that the necessary amount of ventilation is supplied to prevent the collection of moist, stagnant air in any part of the vessel. For preserving the timber, common salt is frequently introduced between the frame joints and between the frame members and the planking and ceiling. Most modern shipbuilders, however, prefer creosote, carbolineum, or some similar compound applied with a brush or old broom to the joints during the process of construction.

On account of differences of opinion recently voiced regarding the advisability of building wooden boats of green timber to meet the present submarine emergency, the following data on the shrinkage of Douglas fir, from a pamphlet by Howard B. Oakleaf, United States forest service, Portland, Ore., are presented:

"Douglas fir does not shrink much, and for this reason it is possible to

FIG. 11—BORING HOLES WITH AN
AIR DRILL

Table I

Average Strength Values for Structural Timbers

GREEN MATERIAL

Taken from United States Forest Service Bulletin 108

Species	Cross section under test. In.	No. of tests	Rings per inch	Moisture content. Per cent	Weight per cu. ft. oven-dry. Lbs.	Fiber stress at elastic limit per sq. in. Lbs.	Modulus of rupture per sq. in. Lbs.	Modulus of Elasticity per sq. in. lbs.	Relative strength based on modulus of rupture. Douglas fir = 100 per cent. Per cent	Relative stiffness based on modulus of elasticity. Douglas fir = 100 per cent. Per cent	Vol. I Less than 1½ in.	Vol. I 1½ in. and over	Vol. II Less than 1½ in.	Vol. II 1½ in. and over	Vol. III Less than 1½ in.	Vol. III 1½ in. and over
Douglas fir	8x16	134	10.9	31.8	28.9 (132)	4,282 (133)	6,605	1,611	100.0	100.0	1.2	0.5	1.7	0.7	10.0	3.3
Long-leaf pine	12x12 10x16 8x16 6x16 6x10	13	14.6 (12)	29.2	35.4	3,855	6,437	1,466	97.4	91.0	0.4	0.2	0.5	0.2	4.0	1.1
Short-leaf pine	8x16 8x14 8x12	33	12.3	48.4	31.4	3,376 (31)	5,948	1,546 (31)	90.0	96.0	0.4	0.1	0.1	0.1	2.4	1.2
Western hemlock	8x16	27	17.6	41.9	28.1	3,761	5,821	1,489	88.1	92.4	0.7	0.7	1.5	0.4	3.4	2.3
Loblolly pine	8x16 5x12	78	6.2 (68)	58.0 (55)	31.2 (55)	3,266	5,568	1,467	84.4	91.1	0.2	0.2	0.3	0.7	4.6	3.7
Western larch	8x16 8x12	43	23.9	50.5	28.7	3,677	5,562	1,364	84.2	84.6	0.9	0.2	2.3	0.6	10.9	1.3
Redwood	8x16 6x12 7x9	30	19.5	90.2	23.3	4,323	5,327	1,202	80.6	74.6	0.9	0.1	1.6	1.3	8.3	3.6
Tamarack	6x12	11	16.7	56.9	29.3	3,231	4,984	1,268	75.5	78.7	0.9	0.4	1.4	0.4	8.4	0.7
Norway pine	6x12	11	13.2	52.1	25.2	2,397	3,767	1,042	57.0	64.7	2.5	1.8	2.8	2.5	14.0	8.7

Note—Subscript numbers indicate number of tests when different from that shown in column "Number of Tests."

Table II

Average Strength Values for Structural Timbers

AIR-SEASONED MATERIAL

Taken from United States Forest Service Bulletin 108

Species	Cross section under test. In.	No. of tests	Rings per inch	Moisture content. Per cent	Weight per cu. ft. oven-dry. Lbs.	Fiber stress at elastic limit per sq. in. Lbs.	Modulus of rupture per sq. in. Lbs.	Modulus of Elasticity per sq. in. lbs.	Relative strength based on modulus of rupture. Douglas fir = 100 per cent. Per cent	Relative stiffness based on modulus of elasticity. Douglas fir = 100 per cent. Per cent	Vol. I Less than 1½ in.	Vol. I 1½ in. and over	Vol. II Less than 1½ in.	Vol. II 1½ in. and over	Vol. III Less than 1½ in.	Vol. III 1½ in. and over
Douglas fir	8x16	64	15.2	20.9	27.8	4,931	7,142	1,641	100.0	100.0	0.5	0.1	1.2	0.2	12.1	0.9
Long-leaf pine	8x16 6x16 6x10	7	12.7	21.6	38.6	3,793 (6)	5,957	1,720	83.6	104.8	None	None	None	None	None	None
Short-leaf pine	8x16 8x14 8x12	9	12.3	16.3	32.1	5,186	7,033	1,782	98.5	108.6	None	None	0.2	0.5	2.8	1.6
Western hemlock	8x16	31	17.5	17.7	28.4	4,828 (30)	7,109	1,805 (30)	99.6	110.0	0.3	0.1	1.6	0.5	8.0	0.7
Loblolly pine	8x16 6x16 6x10 8x8	21	6.5	21.1	33.1	3,706	6,259	1,521	87.7	92.7	0.4	1.1	0.4	0.8	2.8	3.4
Western larch	8x16 8x12	36	23.0	18.2	29.8	3,904	6,534	1,561	91.5	95.1	1.8	0.3	3.2	0.6	19.4	1.6
Redwood	8x16 6x12 7x9	12	18.1	17.3	22.2	3,747 (7)	4,573	946 (7)	64.1	57.6	0.1	None	0.8	0.3	3.0	1.3
Tamarack	6x12	4	16.6	23.4	30.8	3,643	5,865	1,385	82.3	84.4	1.8	None	0.8	None	18.0	0.5
Norway pine	6x12	4	7.8	17.0	26.4	2,928	5,255	1,103	73.7	67.2	3.5	1.5	2.3	0.5	17.5	9.3

Note—Subscript numbers indicate number of tests when different from that shown in column "Number of Tests."

use partially dried material in emergencies, without fear that the additional drying after the material has been shaped will open the seams or cause undesirable stresses in the members. The following figures are given for the information of those desiring to know the amount that Douglas fir will shrink under normal conditions from green to air dry: Radially, 1.52 per cent, tangentially, 2.37 per cent, and longitudinally, 0.0091 per cent." Tables I and II will be found to contain complete data on the strength of the principal American woods used for shipbuilding and other structural purposes. While it is difficult to obtain correct comparisons of the strength properties of structural timbers, yet, from a practical point of view, the full structural sizes furnish the data sought by naval architects and shipbuilders to guide them in their designs.

tions in weight and strength. These variations are considerable in some cases, depending on the quality of the clear wood, as well as on the grade and condition of seasoning of the timber. It is essential that the quality of the timbers of any species be determined by due consideration of these factors, rather than locality of growth, etc.

Table IV probably contains the best available data published in any government bulletin covering the strength of different species of structural timber, The data in this table are taken from United States forest service bulletin No. 108, page 65. This table shows the results of tests on a large number of stringers, similar to ship keelson timbers, of different species, graded by the tentative grading rule of the forest service. All the timbers were practically of the same grade. The modulus of rupture of Douglas fir is given as

cases, the relation between dry weight and strength is erratic.

A knowledge of timber grading is essential to the shipbuilder. Different grading rules are used in different parts of the country, and detailed rule books may be procured from the various lumber associations. On the Pacific coast, the standard grade used at present to secure high grade structural timbers is "Selected Common". This grade covers timbers selected from the grade known as "No 1 Common". No. 1 Common is described as follows:

"This grade shall consist of lengths 8 feet and over (except shorter lengths as ordered) of a quality suitable for ordinary constructional purposes. Will allow a small amount of wane, large sound knots, large pitch pockets, colored sap one-third of the width and one-half the thickness, slight variation in sawing and slight streak of solid heart stain. Defects to be considered in connection with the size of the piece. Discoloration through exposure to the elements or season checks

Table III
Lumber Cut of the United States for 1915 by States

From Data Compiled by the United States Forest Service

State	No. of mills active	Production in thousand board feet	State	No. of mills active	Production in thousand board feet
Washington	440	3,950,000	New York	1,600	475,000
Louisiana	500	3,900,000	Ohio	850	400,000
Mississippi	1,250	2,200,000	Missouri	850	350,000
North Carolina	2,900	2,000,000	Indiana	750	350,000
Texas	500	1,850,000	Montana	104	328,000
Arkansas	1,150	1,800,000	Vermont	500	260,000
Oregon	410	1,690,000	Massachusetts	400	250,000
Alabama	1,350	1,500,000	Oklahoma	225	230,000
Virginia	2,400	1,500,000	Maryland	400	165,000
Wisconsin	600	1,300,000	Illinois	350	110,000
California	150	1,130,000	Connecticut	200	90,000
Florida	400	1,110,000	Colorado	144	79,500
Michigan	600	1,100,000	Arizona	14	75,915
Minnesota	450	1,100,000	New Mexico	43	65,787
West Virginia	950	1,100,000	New Jersey	250	40,000
Maine	900	1,000,000	Iowa	125	35,000
Georgia	1,400	1,000,000	Delaware	75	25,000
Pennsylvania	1,900	950,000	South Dakota	29	23,800
South Carolina	800	800,000	Wyoming	74	17,400
Tennessee	1,800	800,000	Rhode Island	25	15,000
Idaho	210	777,000	Utah	73	10,892
Kentucky	1,300	560,000			
New Hampshire	500	500,000	Totals	29,941	37,013,294

For Tables I and II we are indebted to the West Coast Lumbermen's association, Seattle, O. P. M. Goss, consulting engineer. In the preparation of the tables, showing the various properties of structural timbers, every effort was made to obtain the most reliable and up-to-date figures. In all comparisons, consideration was given to the size of the timbers, general quality, moisture condition and other factors which affect the strength. Many publications have presented data containing strength values for structural timbers, but in many cases the timbers have been unlike in grades and have varied materially in moisture content. Due to such variations, comparisons, in many cases have been very misleading. This point has been recognized in preparing the accompanying data, and every effort was made to eliminate comparisons that were not on the same basis.

All species of timber show varia-

6919 pounds per square inch; the corresponding figure for long leaf pine is 6140 pounds per square inch.

The dry weight of small, clear specimens, particularly for wood containing little or no resinous substance, is a definite indication of the strength of the wood fibre. This fact is shown for Douglas fir in United States forest service bulletin No. 108, in which it is stated that with an increase in dry weight of from 19 to 36 pounds per cubic foot, there is an accompanying increase in strength (modulus of rupture) of from 5500 to 10,500 pounds per square inch. These figures indicate increases of 47.2 and 47.7 per cent respectively for weight and strength, based on the maximum values. In timbers of structural sizes, however, such as are used in shipbuilding, this law does not hold good on account of the influence of the knots on the strength. In such

not exceeding in length one-half the width of the piece, shall not be deemed a defect excluding lumber from this grade, if otherwise conforming to the grade of No. 1 Common."

From the foregoing specifications for No. 1 Common, the following specification for Selected Common, suitable for high class constructional purposes, including bridge timbers, floor joists, ship timbers, etc., designed to carry heavy loads most satisfactorily, is deduced:

"Selected Common is a grade selected from No. 1 Common and shall consist of lumber free from defects that materially impair the strength of the piece, well manufactured and suitable for high class constructional and structural purposes."

Considerable more information might be presented on the strength and physical characteristics of ship timbers, but enough has been included to embrace the fundamental facts, and for more exhaustive data the reader is referred to civil engineering hand books and to

1—Cutting the tree
2—Logs on car ready to go to beach
3—Skidding logs to river
4—Future ship timbers

FIG. 12—TYPICAL LUMBERING SCENES IN THE NORTHWEST

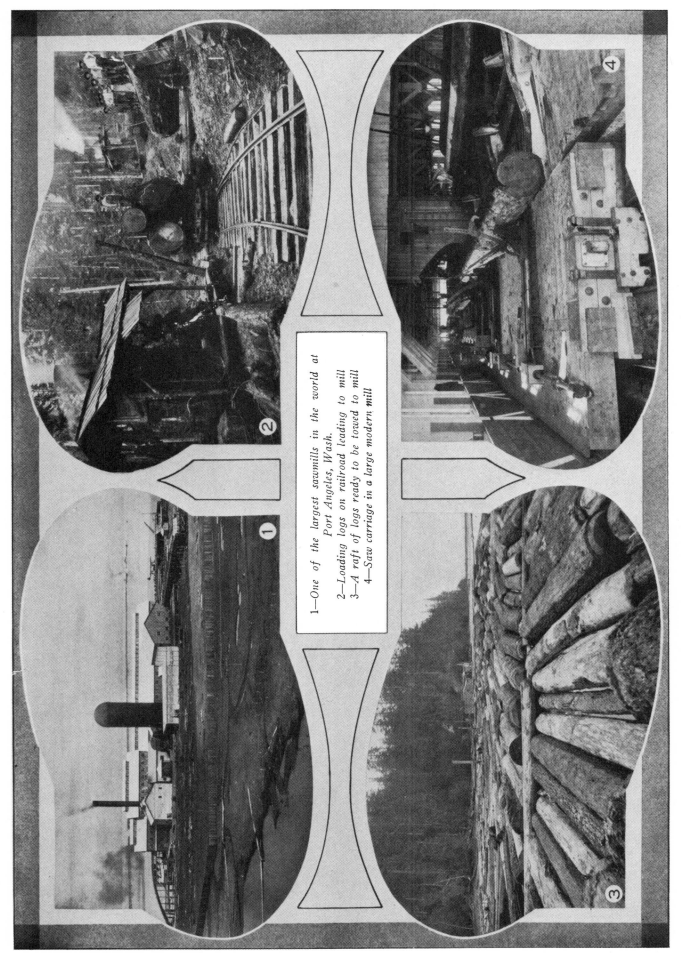

1—One of the largest sawmills in the world at Port Angeles, Wash.
2—Loading logs on railroad leading to mill
3—A raft of logs ready to be towed to mill
4—Saw carriage in a large modern mill

FIG. 13—WEST COAST LUMBERING REQUIRES SPECIAL, HEAVY DUTY EQUIPMENT

the various special booklets on structural timber, such as that issued by the West Coast Lumbermen's association. It might be added, however, that a safe fibre stress for fir or pine, is considered to be from 1600 to 1800 pounds per square inch in tension, 1600 pounds for compression parallel to the grain, and 400 pounds for compression across the grain: The weaknesses introduced by the practice of sawing out the bilge turns in the frame timbers of large ships are indicated by the great variation in the last two sets of figures.

How Timbers are Shaped

Before going on into the design and construction of ships in detail, it is advisable briefly to consider the methods of shaping and fashioning timbers for ship construction and also the principal methods of fastening the various elements together. The data about to be presented is of a purely general character. More detailed methods of working up timbers and fastenings will be considered later.

Generally speaking, timbers are shaped by sawing, chopping, planing and boring. As far as possible, in modern wooden shipyards, machines are supplanting hand labor for all of these operations. Band saws or jig saws, together with common circular saws are used for a great variety of operations. Air-driven boring augers are used and special machines have been developed for beveling timbers and performing other operations peculiar to shipbuilding. In many cases, however, hand tools must be used, as for instance in dubbing-off the inside of the hull preparatory to laying the ceiling. For many operations such as this, the adz is indispensable. For rough hewing, axes are employed, while hand planes, bits, chisels, and all the tools found in the carpenter's kit also are utilized.

For fastenings, dowels, treenails, drift bolts, spikes and screw bolts are employed. The various pieces may also be

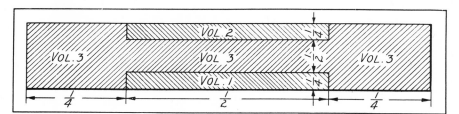

FIG. 14—DIVISION OF STRINGER INTO VOLUMES FOR CONSIDERATION
OF POSITIONS OF KNOTS—SEE TABLES I AND II

scarfed, that is, beveled together, so as to add to the strength of the joint.

Treenails are usually 1¼ inches in diameter and from 26 to 30 inches long. They are made of hard wood, usually locust, and are used chiefly for fastening the planking and ceiling to the frames. For this purpose a hole the scant diameter of the treenail is bored in the members to be fastened and the treenail is driven home with an air hammer. After it is in place, it is cut off, split on the end, and wedged to a tight fit. The subsequent action of the water is supposed to swell the treenail and make it fit tighter.

Although treenails are used extensively in modern shipbuilding, there is doubt as to their efficiency after the ship has had an opportunity to work in a seaway. Undoubtedly, however, they were employed in the construction of the ark, for want of knowledge of more modern fastenings, and this is a sufficient recommendation for their continued use in the eyes of many old-line shipbuilders. The chief virtue of treenails seems to lie in the fact that they work with the ship, and therefore do not present as unyielding a resistance as a steel fastening.

To supplement treenails, however, in fastening the main members of wooden ships together, steel or iron drift-bolts are used. Usually they are about 1-inch in diameter. They are generally driven by air hammers in holes bored ⅟₁₆-inch smaller in diameter than the bolt. Although the difference between the size of the hole and that of the bolt is small, they hold tenaciously, especially when the ship is new. It is said that drift-bolts driven 3 feet into a fir timber hold so fast that they break in tension before they pull out. Wherever possible such bolts are driven through and clenched on steel rings in the inside.

For "sticking" the planking to the frames and other preliminary fastenings, as well as for securing the deck planks, galvanized standard ship spikes are used. Usually they are ½-inch square and 8 or 10 inches long. Screw bolts also are used for some forms of fastenings, as well as bolts fitted with washers and nuts. The latter may be taken up from time to time as required.

Tests of Spikes

Some tests of spikes were made at the Seattle testing laboratory of the

United States forest service recently, from which the following conclusions were drawn:

1—The form of the point of the common spike is such that it inclines not to follow the hole.

2—If the holes are not too large and the spikes follow the holes closely, the resistance to withdrawal usually will be increased.

3—If spikes do not follow the holes, the resistance to withdrawal may be greatly reduced.

4—Spikes driven close to the holes, but not into them, will have their resistance lowered.

In modern wooden vessels built on the coasts of the United States, considerable use is made of edge-bolting to fasten the various keel and keelson elements and the strakes of ceiling together. Edge bolting means fastening the pieces together longitudinally. In other words, the ceiling strakes are bolted through and through to each other, as well as being bolted to the frame timbers. There is no doubt that this form of fastening adds greatly to the strength of the hull structure, particularly in a longitudinal direction, offering resistance to hogging strains. In fact, some experts go as far as to say that the edge-bolting is all that prevents the largest of wooden ships from breaking-up in a seaway. This is probably an exaggeration, although it has been demonstrated that timbers well edge-bolted at least approximate the strength of single pieces of the size of the members so combined.

Table IV
Average Strength Values for Structural Timbers
(Grade 1, Tentative Grading Rules, U. S. Forest Service)
GREEN MATERIAL
Results Taken from United States Forest Service Bulletin 108, Page 65, Table 8

Species	No. of tests	Fiber stress at elastic limit per sq. in. Pounds	Modulus of rupture per sq. in. Pounds	Modulus of elasticity per sq. in. 1,000 pounds	Relative strength based on modulus of rupture. Douglas fir = 100 per cent. Per cent	Relative stiffness based on modulus of elasticity. Douglas fir = 100 per cent. Per cent
Douglas fir	81	4,402	6,919	1,643	100.0	100.0
Longleaf pine	17	3,734	6,140	1,463	88.7	89.0
Loblolly pine	45	3,513	5,898	1,535	85.3	93.4
Shortleaf pine	35	3,318	5,849	1,525	84.5	92.8
Western hemlock	26	3,689	5,615	1,481	81.1	90.2
Western larch	45	3,662	5,479	1,365	79.2	83.1
Tamarack	9	3,151	5,469	1,276	79.0	77.7
Redwood	21	4,031	4,932	1,097	71.3	66.8
Norway pine	17	3,082	4,821	1,373	69.6	83.6

FIG. 15—A WELL LAID OUT WOODEN SHIPYARD LOCATED IN THE CENTER OF A LARGE CITY

CHAPTER III

Layout and Equipment of Wooden Shipbuilding Plants

IN THE two previous chapters in this book, the general possibilities and limitations of wooden ships were discussed and the structural characteristics of ship timber were studied in detail. Before the actual work of building the ship can commence, there is still another problem to be disposed of—the shipyard must be planned and equipped. If the prospective builder is going into the construction of wooden ships on a permanent basis, this problem is perhaps the most important one he will be called upon to solve. Mistakes in the design or method of building a given hull can be rectified when the next ship is laid down; blunders in the layout or equipment of the shipyard can seldom be corrected, except at prohibitive expense. Like most other old saws, the adage about the poor workman always blaming his tools is only a half truth; good workmanship demands the use of the best tools and is intolerant of slipshod equipment. Therefore, the shipbuilder who starts out with a half-baked, poorly laid out, pinched and skimped plant, is saddling himself with a handicap that may later spell ruin. The impression is all too prevalent that a well planned, thoroughly equipped plant, carefully arranged and organized, is relatively unnecessary for building wooden ships. Quite the reverse is true, and a study of the plants that have built ships continuously for a generation or more, through good times and bad, reveals the fact that they are all as completely equipped for their task as any steel shipyard. In fact, one of the unfortunate results of the present boom is the multiplication of hay-wire yards on both eastern and western coasts. If wooden shipbuilding is to establish itself permanently, the idea that anybody's back lot will do for a building site and a chest of carpenter's tools for equipment, must be definitely abandoned. Wooden shipbuilding is no longer a haven for irresponsible promoters. Success in this field demands money, brains, skill and experience—the more the better.

The location of the yard is the first phase of the problem to be considered. Four factors govern the selection of the site: The supply of labor, the cost of the land, the contour of the ground and the depth of the water. Labor supply and real estate prices are complementary; where labor is abundant, property is expensive, and where land is cheap the supply of labor is dubious. The builder must compromise these conflicting elements to the best of his judgment and ability, remembering that a busy yard may carry a high overhead, but no plant can be run without men. It is significant that the most successful of the modern wooden shipbuilding plants on the Pacific coast are located in or near large cities. This would indicate that labor supply is the controlling factor.

In selecting a site for wooden shipbuilding, the slope and contour of the ground is important. Preferably, the ships should be built on dry land that has just sufficient natural slope to permit the laying of the keel blocks conveniently. There also must be level property for the construction of buildings and the storage of lumber. These conditions are not always easily fulfilled, although they are found in many of the oldest and most successful yards. In some cases, where long tide flats are encountered, filling has been resorted to, and although it is an expensive process, an ideal site can be created in this manner. An example

FIG. 16—ELECTRICALLY-DRIVEN, TRAVELING DERRICK SETTING FRAMES IN A WOODEN SHIPYARD

FIG. 17—WOODEN SHIPYARD LOCATED ON NATURALLY SLOPING GROUND WITH AN ABUNDANCE OF ROOM

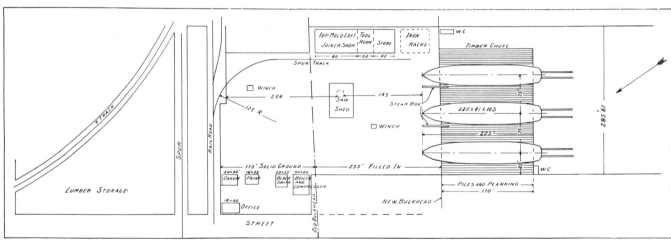

FIG. 18—A SMALL YARD LAID OUT ON LONG NARROW STRIP OF GROUND

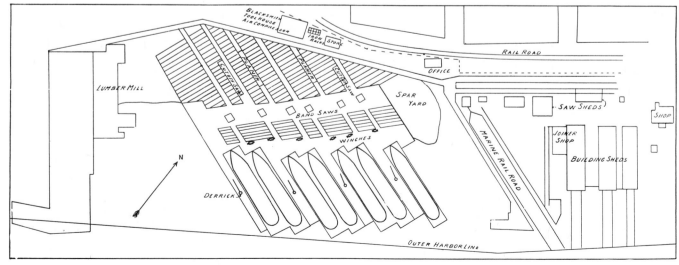

FIG. 19—YARD LAID OUT ON IRREGULAR PLOT OF GROUND

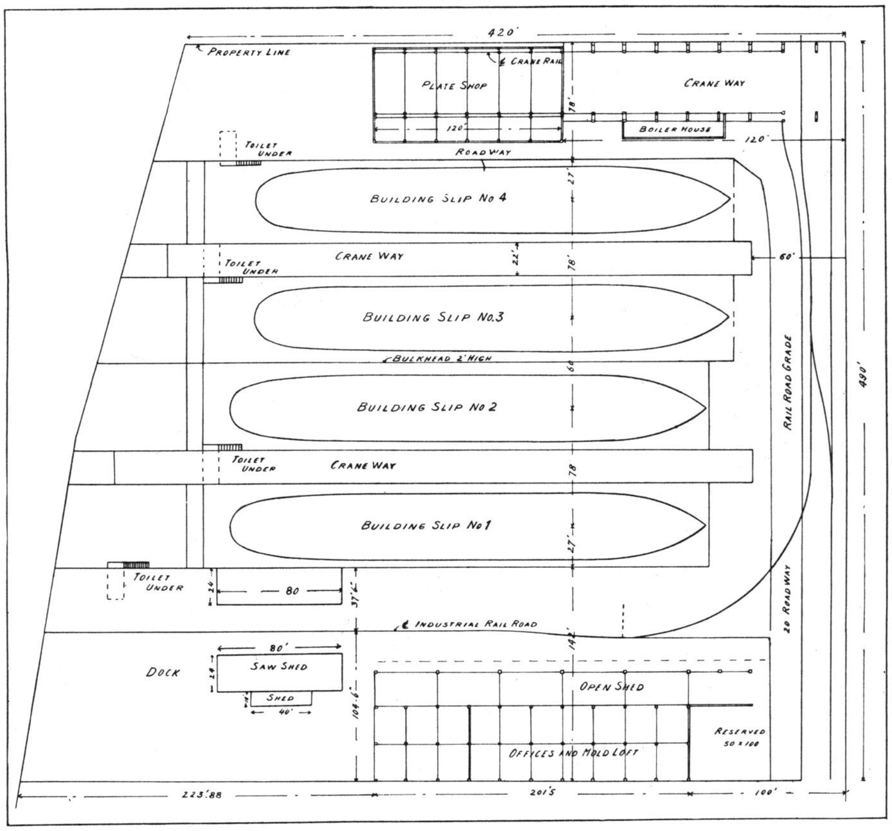

of the relative importance of properly preparing the site is found in the estimates for a small California yard, in which the cost of buildings is given as $9280 and the yard work at $16,520, including $4720 for filling. In some Pacific coast yards where natural ground conditions are unfavorable, the building ways, framing stages and even the foundations for buildings and lumber storage have been placed on piles. On fresh-water rivers, safe from the ravages of the toredo, this procedure is not so objectionable as on salt water, but under all circumstances it is subject to criticism on account of being temporary and a source of continual expense for renewals. This practice can be defended only in cases where the builder feels his business is so purely transient that the expense of filling-in permanent foundations or paying enough for a suitable natural site, is unjustified.

In many wooden shipyards too little consideration has been given the influence of the shape of the property on the progress of the material through the plant. Many yards, especially some of the newer ones, are laid out with no thought whatever, apparently, to the labor that might be saved by properly and thoughtfully routing the work. The principles of straight-line progress that are so ingrained in the metalworking industries and most other productive establishments, have been completely overlooked. The result is chaos and a tremendous waste of money. This comes from the practice of throwing the yards together rather than having them designed by a competent, experienced engineer.

If routing alone is to be considered, a long, narrow yard, in which

FIG. 20—YARD WITH FOUR BUILDING SLIPS COMPACTLY ARRANGED ON CITY PROPERTY

FIG. 21—A STEEL FRAMED REVOLVING CRANE FOR WOODEN SHIPYARD

FIG. 22—MILL CONTAINING SAWS AND WOODWORKING MACHINERY

the raw material comes in at one end and proceeds in a straight line to the building ways at the other, is ideal. This arrangement can seldom be realized, and the next choice is a rectangular yard in which the material flows around only one corner and does not double back at any point. Regardless of the shape of the plot, however, and the limitations of property lines, a skilled designer can so arrange the equipment as to get the most out of the situation at hand and avoid waste in handling materials.

The accompanying illustrations, Figs. 18, 19 and 20, illustrate some of the principles of yard arrangement. Fig. 18 shows a small yard for three ships designed by Martin C. Erismann, engineer. In this case, a long, narrow piece of ground was available and a straight-line plant was the result.

Fig. 19, detailing the yard of the Grays Harbor Motorship Corp., Aberdeen, Wash., shows what can be done with a comparatively shallow, irregular plot on which a large number of building slips must be placed. In this case, extra room and proper routing is obtained by placing the slips at an acute angle with the harbor line. The advantages of angular layouts of this general character have long been understood by industrial engineers.

Getting the Most Out of City Property

Fig. 20 shows what can be done on comparatively restricted ground area in the heart of a city. In this case, four building slips for ships of the largest size are provided, together with ample room for shops of a more elaborate character than are usually found around wooden shipbuilding plants, yet the plant is not over-crowded. The lumber moves across

the yard from south to north and is properly distributed by means of the traveling cranes between the first and second and third and fourth slips. The steel fittings, which are made-up in the plate shop, move in the opposite direction. This plant is operated by Supple & Ballin, Portland, Oreg. How the arrangement works out in actual practice is shown clearly in Fig. 15, which gives a good general view of the yard under operating conditions.

The patent advantages of an almost perfect natural site, with unlimited room, are shown in Fig. 17, which illustrates the yard of the Winslow Marine Railway & Shipbuilding Co., Winslow, Wash. In this case, piling or filling are unnecessary, for the ground has the correct natural slope for laying keel blocks and the water deepens rapidly from the shore. The ways are laid out along the shore and

covered by sheds, with the shops, mill, etc., immediately in the rear.

The cost of wooden shipyards varies, of course, within wide limits, depending on the locality, price of the ground, number of building slips and the completeness of the shop and yard equipment. In altogether too many cases the latter item is dangerously slighted. Probably $45,000 represents the minimum for three slips, and in this case the margin is hardly comfortable. From this figure, the investment ranges up to $500,000. While no definite suggestions can be given where so many variables are to be considered, it is safe to say that a reasonable sum invested in the plant and its equipment makes for permanent success.

Proper Design and Layout

This chapter is concerned with the general phases of yard design and layout. Details, such as the construction, slope and arrangement of the keel blocks and the foundations of the building slips will be treated later in the chapters devoted to construction procedure. Various methods of laying out the building slips are suggested by the drawings, Figs. 18, 19 and 20, previously mentioned.

In the north Pacific coast region, on Puget sound and the Columbia river, the question of protecting the building slips with sheds is a moot one. There is no doubt the protection of the work from the weather during construction tends to add to the life of the vessel, and that from the standpoint of the comfort of the workmen and their efficiency, especially in the winter time when rain is frequent, sheds are desirable. On the other hand, they add greatly to the cost of the yard, and this is the principal reason why so much

FIG. 23—CUT-OFF AND BAND SAW SHEDS IN A WESTERN SHIPYARD

Table V
Cost of Buildings, etc., for Small Yard Shown in Fig. 18

Three Building Slips

Mold loft, 2-story, 45 x 100 feet, bottom floor containing joiner shop, 45 x 80; tool room, 45 x 30 and store room, 45 x 40	$4,500
Office, 18 x 35 feet	1,000
Blacksmith shop, 20 x 25 feet	350
Oakum store, 20 x 30 feet	400
Boiler house and compressor room, 30 x 40 feet	800
Steel storage racks	150
Paint shop, 18 x 25 feet	150
Saw sheds, 45 x 70 feet	250
Steam boxes, two 3 x 3 x 50 feet	180
Piping for water and air	1,500
Spur track	800
Filling and bulkheading	4,720
Ways, piling and flooring	10,000
Miscellaneous	1,000
Total	$25,800

Table VI
Equipment for Small Shipyard Shown in Fig. 18

One 48-inch band saw	$2,600
One 20-horsepower motor for band saw	421
Two 30-inch saws for loft and joiner shop	330
Two motors for 30-inch saws	200
One circular table saw	425
One buzz knee planer or 24-inch jointer	700
One bolt cutter	350
Grindstones and emery wheels	200
Mauls, dogs, chains, rope, peavys	2,000
Forty jacks	320
Clamps, screws, Nelson iron	1,000
Two anvils	150
Two forges	200
Two steam winches	3,000
One drill press	450
One air compressor	2,696
Six 90-lb. air hammers	300
One extra heavy hammer	175
Six wood boring machines	450
Air hose	300
Motors	1,000
Boiler, pumps, etc.	1,500
Miscellaneous	1,000
Total	$19,767

work is being done out-of-doors on both coasts. A well designed, light, permanent building-shed big enough to protect a hull up to 300 feet in length, is shown in Fig. 34. Such a shed costs over $20,000. This shed is provided with a monorail crane system for economically handling materials. Some modern wooden shipbuilders have not provided sheds because they preclude the use of cranes that are considered to be of an unusually efficient type.

This brings us to the consideration of the equipment necessary for economically handling materials, which, with the tools required for working-up timbers, constitutes the bulk of the machinery in a wooden shipyard. In many wooden shipyards, as previously suggested, the problem of handling lumber and other materials has been given scant consideration. Too often the traditions of the logging camp and the old-line sawmill have been handed on to the shipyard without any thought of the difference in the problems to be solved.

In the smaller yards, however, where the overhead soon becomes serious, simplicity of equipment is permissible. In such cases, a small hoisting engine or two and a few hundred feet of wire rope are about all that are required for handling timbers, supplemented by a few dollies or lumber trucks. The timbers are handled by skidding them from place to place in the conventional lumberman's fashion.

Fig. 28 shows the hoisting and skidding equipment for a Pacific coast shipyard with three building ways. In this case the outfit consists of one double-drum and one single-drum

FIG. 24—GENERAL VIEW OF A SEATTLE SHIPYARD SHOWING BEVELING MACHINE, ARRANGEMENT OF DERRICKS, BUILDING SLIPS, ETC.

FIG. 25—WOODWORKING MACHINERY IN A PUGET SOUND SHIPYARD

FIG. 26—BANDSAWING BEVELS IN A SOUTH ATLANTIC SHIPYARD.   FIG. 27—DERRICKS AND HOISTING ENGINE
IN A SOUTHERN YARD

FIG. 28—TIMBER HAULING ENGINES IN A GRAYS HARBOR SHIPYARD.   FIG. 29—DRIVING PILES FOR BUILDING
WAYS IN A GEORGIA SHIPYARD

FIG. 30—GENERAL ARRANGEMENT OF BUILDING WAYS SHOWING VESSELS IN VARIOUS STAGES OF CONSTRUCTION.
FIG. 31—PORTABLE ELECTRICALLY DRIVEN PLANER. FIG. 32—BAND SAWING EQUIPMENT IN A PACIFIC COAST
YARD. FIG. 33—TRAVELING TABLE FOR HANDLING TIMBER AROUND MACHINES. FIG. 34—A BUILDING
SHED PROTECTS THE WORK FROM THE WEATHER

hoisting engine with a vertical nigger-head for handling the manila haul-back line. The steam is supplied by a vertical donkey boiler 5 feet in diameter and 8 feet high. It carries about 80 pounds pressure and burns wood refuse from the yard that other-wise would go to waste. Almost the whole expense of operating this rig, therefore, is the wages of the engineer, $4.50 per day. A ½-inch wire rope is used for hauling the timbers. This equipment serves three hulls handling all the timbers for frames, keelsons, ceiling, etc. The cost of such an outfit should not exceed $1500. Frequently second-hand contractor's equipment is purchased at low prices. The services of the donkey engine are usually supplemented by a few rough timber derricks, as shown in Fig. 27.

In more elaborately equipped yards, and in most cases where thoroughly satisfactory results are desired, some form of crane equipment is provided. In cases where there are building sheds, rope or electrically driven I-beam monorail hoists running the full length of the shed have been found to fill the bill. Where the work is out in the open, traveling cranes of the types shown in Figs. 16 and 21 are most frequently employed.

Two Types of Cranes

Both of these cranes were designed specially to meet conditions in wooden shipbuilding yards. The main framing of the crane shown in Fig. 16 is wood; the one illustrated in Fig. 21 has a steel frame. Both cranes are simply variations of the traveling derrick.

The timber-framed derrick shown in Fig. 16, sometimes called a "monstrosity", has a boom 72 feet in length, set on a base 30 feet above the ground. It will handle 7 tons, and might be termed a shear legs on wheels. It is electrically operated, the power being supplied through a looped, insulated cable that slides on a wire stretched alongside the runway. To give the machine stability, the hoisting machinery is placed on the lower of the two platforms shown in Fig. 16. A 50-horsepower motor geared to a 3-drum hoist is provided. The hoist also is equipped with a small niggerhead for skidding light timbers. The operator's cab is on the upper platform, at the foot of the derrick. The foot-spread, or gage of track on which the crane runs, is 35 feet. One such crane will serve two building slips.

The crane shown in Fig. 21 is mounted on a turntable that permits the boom to swing through 360 degrees, an advantage the timber-framed traveler just described does not possess. The boom in the case of the revolving crane shown in Fig. 21 has a reach of 50 feet.

For handling light timbers in single pieces, ordinary lumber dollies and wide-tired four-wheel trucks are used in great profusion in wooden shipyards. These vehicles usually are of the simplest character, consisting of nothing more than a timber frame to which the wheels and axles are bolted. They may be moved by man power, although horses are usually employed. In some of the more progressive yards, small gasoline-driven tractors have been introduced, making it possible to handle the lumber trucks in trains.

Woodworking Machinery

The equipment required for working-up timbers, including the band saws, cut-off saws, jig saws, planing machines, automatic beveling machines, etc., must be carefully arranged so the work can be gotten out expeditiously with a minimum of rehandling. There are two general methods of arranging this equipment. In some yards it is grouped together in a mill located, usually, at a convenient point in front of the building ways. In other yards, the apparatus is scattered among a number of small saw sheds, on the unit principle. In the latter case, each building slip is provided with an individual saw outfit, located, generally, at the head of the ways. A mill in which all the sawing equipment is grouped together is shown in Fig. 22. A pair of individual saw sheds of the unit type is shown in Fig. 23. In this illustration, the cut-off saw, with derrick and hoisting engine for handling timbers, is in the background, with the band-saw shed, in which the curved frame sections are shaped, in the right foreground. The simple and inexpensive character of the equipment is clearly shown. A searchlight for night work is mounted on the band-saw shed.

In order to give a concrete idea of the equipment required for wooden shipbuilding and its cost, Tables V and VI are presented, giving the cost of buildings and equipment for the 3-way yard shown in Fig. 18. The prices are based on quotations in April, 1917. The equipment listed may be considered a minimum for the work to be done, and if more money were available considerable apparatus could be added, such as cranes, automatic beveling machines, etc. The total cost of the three major items is as follows: Buildings, $9280; yard work, $16,520; machinery and tools, $19,767; total, $45,567, exclusive of real estate, supplies or working capital.

CHAPTER IV

Details of Different Types of Wooden Vessels

AFTER providing for the layout, equipment and organization of his plant, the wooden shipbuilder turns naturally to a consideration of the structural details of the various types of vessels he may be called upon to turn out. The successful builder is familiar with all kinds of ships, and is broad minded enough to realize that valuable suggestions may be obtained from a study of even the so-called freak designs. He knows also that before he can go ahead with the details of his building operations, he must become thoroughly familiar with the general outlines of a large number of boats. It is logical, therefore, to insert a chapter at this point in our book which will set forth the salient facts regarding a number of different wooden ship models in such a manner that the reader may readily compare the various designs. This can best be done by presenting a number of detailed drawings, supplemented by such descriptive text as may be necessary. The drawings and reproductions of photographs, however, really tell the story and they should be studied carefully.

The Conventional Type

Fig. 5 shows a cross section of a modern American wooden ship of the conventional type. The salient features of this type were discussed in Chapter I.

Details of an old English ship also were presented. The ship shown in Fig. 5 is 48 feet beam and about 275 feet in length. Her floors are 18 inches deep. The keel is 18 x 20 inches. The bottom planking is 4½ x 14 inches. The ceiling over the floors is 10 x 16 inches and over the bilges 12 x 12 inches. The backbone consists of nine keelsons 20 inches square surmounted by a 20 x 24-inch rider keelson. The keelson assembly is connected to the lower and upper deck beams by means of 14 x 14-inch stanchions. Both sets of deck beams are 14 x 16 inches in cross section. These few dimensions are presented to give an idea of the size of timbers used in the construction of vessels of this class.

This type of ship was developed and brought to a high state of perfection on the Pacific coast where it is employed principally in the lumber carrying trade. Experience has shown, however, that vessels of this general design—they are called steam schooners on the west coast—are not suited to long off-shore voyages or for carrying general cargo. Their hull construction is too shallow for one thing.

Furthermore, although the builders of these boats are exceedingly lavish in the use of timber, their strength is not all that could be desired. It has been found that when running light in heavy seas they have a tendency to hog. As a matter of fact, what really happens is that owing to their transverse weakness, the floors are bulged up from the bottom, sometimes seriously distorting the hull structure. The only way the old line builders have found to correct this tendency to hog or bulge is to use heavier ceiling and add more lumber to the hull structure. This, however, is hardly a logical method of attacking the problem.

Weakness Studied

The problem of overcoming the inherent weaknesses of wooden ship construction has been the object of close study by a large number of naval architects for a couple of years—ever since the revival in wooden shipbuilding set in in earnest. As a result of this intensive effort, a number of somewhat modified designs have been evolved, covering the construction of wooden vessels for deep sea service. The latest designs provide for boats up to 308 feet in length and of 4000 tons capacity. In some of them steel is employed extensively.

The question of using steel reinforcing in some form to counteract some of the characteristic weaknesses of wooden hulls is a moot one. Some builders, particularly of the older generation, claim it is not practicable to fasten wood and steel members together in a satisfactory manner. It is interesting to observe, how-

FIG. 35—A 5-MASTED, TOPMAST WOODEN AUXILIARY SCHOONER BUILT AT A PROMINENT PACIFIC COAST SHIPYARD

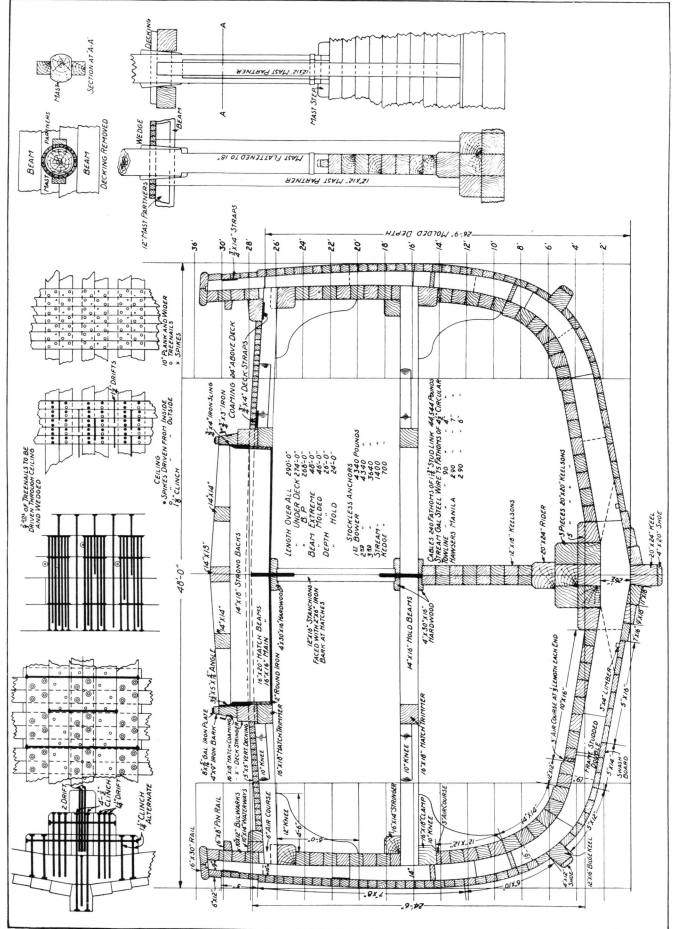

FIG. 36–MIDSHIP SECTION AND CONSTRUCTION DETAILS OF A 290-FOOT, 5-MASTED TOPMAST AUXILIARY SCHOONER

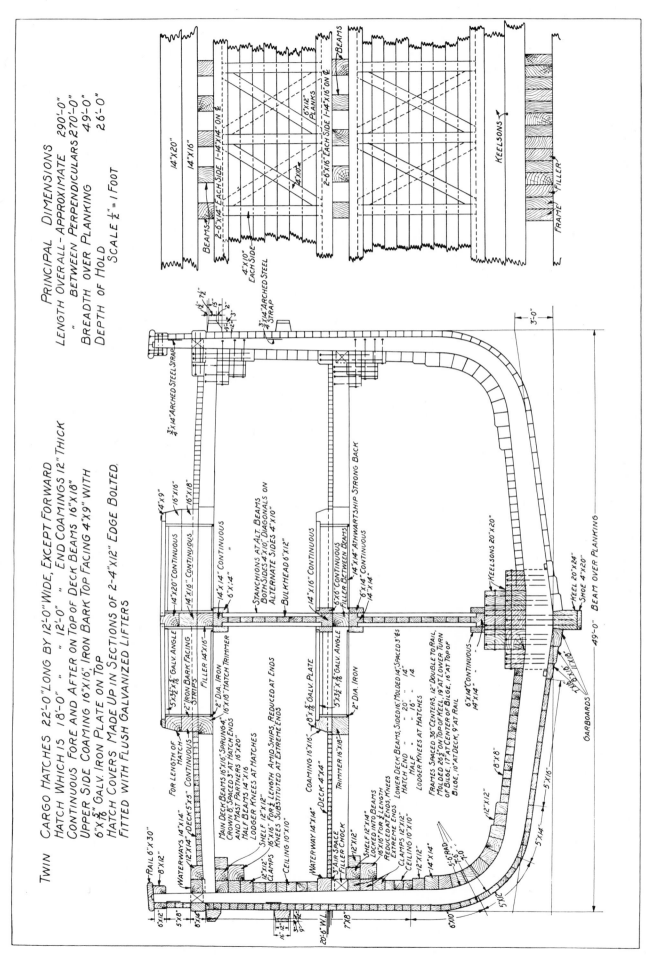

FIG. 37—MIDSHIP SECTION AND CONSTRUCTION DETAILS OF 4000-TON WOODEN STEAMER DESIGNED FOR CONSTRUCTION ON THE PACIFIC COAST

PRINCIPAL DIMENSIONS

LENGTH OVERALL-APPROXIMATE 290'-0"
" BETWEEN PERPENDICULARS 270'-0"
BREADTH OVER PLANKING 49'-0"
DEPTH OF HOLD 26'-0"

SCALE ¼"=1 FOOT

TWIN CARGO HATCHES 22'-0" LONG BY 12'-0" WIDE, EXCEPT FORWARD
HATCH WHICH IS 18'-0" " 12'-0" " END COAMINGS 12" THICK
CONTINUOUS FORE AND AFTER ON TOP OF DECK BEAMS 16"x18"
UPPER SIDE COAMING 16"x16", IRON BARK TOP FACING 4"x9" WITH
6"x5/8" GALV. IRON PLATE ON TOP
HATCH COVERS MADE UP IN SECTIONS OF 2-4"x12" EDGE BOLTED.
FITTED WITH FLUSH GALVANIZED LIFTERS

FIG. 38—A 5-MASTED WOODEN AUXILIARY SCHOONER UNDERGOING HER TRIAL TRIP

ever, that virtually all of the larger vessels under construction on the Pacific coast at the present time are reinforced with steel in one form or another. If current practice is any guide, it may safely be stated that steel reinforcement is necessary for hulls over 275 feet in length and exceeding, say, 3500 tons dead weight.

Various types of steel reinforcing are employed. In some cases, this consists simply of deck straps, with steel lined hatch combings. The deck straps usually are nothing more than flats ¾ inch thick and 4 inches wide riveted together at the ends.

The design worked out by Theodore E. Ferris for the standard wooden vessels for the United States Emergency Fleet Corp. provides for a system of diagonal steel strapping, somewhat similar to that illustrated in Fig. 6, in the first chapter of this book. The straps in the government boats are ½ x 4 inches in cross section and, of course, extend around and under the turn of the bilge. They are riveted at the top to ¾ x 8-inch steel chord. The straps are arranged in the form of a diagonal lattice and are riveted together where they cross. They are lined up to meet the top chord at every other frame space and are fastened to the frame timbers by 8-inch bolts. It is said this form of strapping for a 281-foot government boat costs $8000, including $5000 for labor. Two other forms of steel strapping are in general use on the Pacific coast at the present time. One style, designed by M. R. Ward, general manager, Grays Harbor Ship Building Co., Aberdeen, Wash., consists of two arches of ¾ x 14-inch universal plates let into the sides of the frames and securely bolted in place. The other type, designed by Fred A. Ballin, Supple & Ballin, Portland, Oreg., involves the construction of a

steel bulwark or topside over the upper ends of the frame timbers. The steel topside construction is riveted to a deck stringer plate of suitable dimensions. The details of these two latter forms of strapping will be described later in this chapter.

Standard Designs

Modern designers, however, do not depend entirely on steel reinforcing for strengthening naturally weak wooden hulls. In the newer types of ships, the general arrangement of the hull structure has been materially modified and the distribution of timbers radically altered. The details of three types of modern Pacific coast construction are presented in Figs. 36, 37 and 40. A study of these three cross sections presents interesting contrasts. Before their details are taken up, however, it would

be well to get clearly in mind the outward appearance and general arrangement of modern wooden vessels.

The outboard profiles and deck plans of three ships of standard type, therefore, are presented in Figs. 41, 42 and 43. These are all full-power boats. Auxiliary craft are shown in Figs. 35, 38, 39, 44 and 45. Fig. 44 shows the inboard profile of a typical 5-masted, 290-foot, topmast schooner, the general arrangement of which is indicated in Fig. 35.

The vessel shown in Fig. 41 is more or less like that designed for the United States Emergency Fleet Corp. It is of 4000 tons deadweight capacity, however, and is designed to burn oil fuel. This vessel is 265 feet in length, 43 beam and 26 feet deep. Power is derived from a triple expansion steam engine of about 1500 horsepower, placed amidships. It drives a single screw. The hull structure is divided by five watertight bulkheads arranged as shown in the outboard profile, Fig. 41. The cargo capacity of this vessel in cubic feet is as follows:

	Cubic feet
'Tween deck forward	27,600
Lower hold forward	66,800
'Tween deck aft	32,200
Lower hold aft	26,500
Main deck house	7,000
Total	160,100

A steel cargo boom for handling weights of the heavier character is provided forward.

A somewhat similar vessel, but more of the Great Lakes type, with the engines aft, is shown in Fig. 42. This ship, which is 300 feet long, 45 feet wide and 27 feet deep, has a deadweight capacity of 4500 tons. The machinery is practically a duplicate of that installed in the vessel shown in Fig. 41. In this case there are only four watertight bulkheads. Access to the main

FIG. 39—THREE-THOUSAND TON, 4-MASTED SCHOONER BUILT AT SEATTLE, WASH.

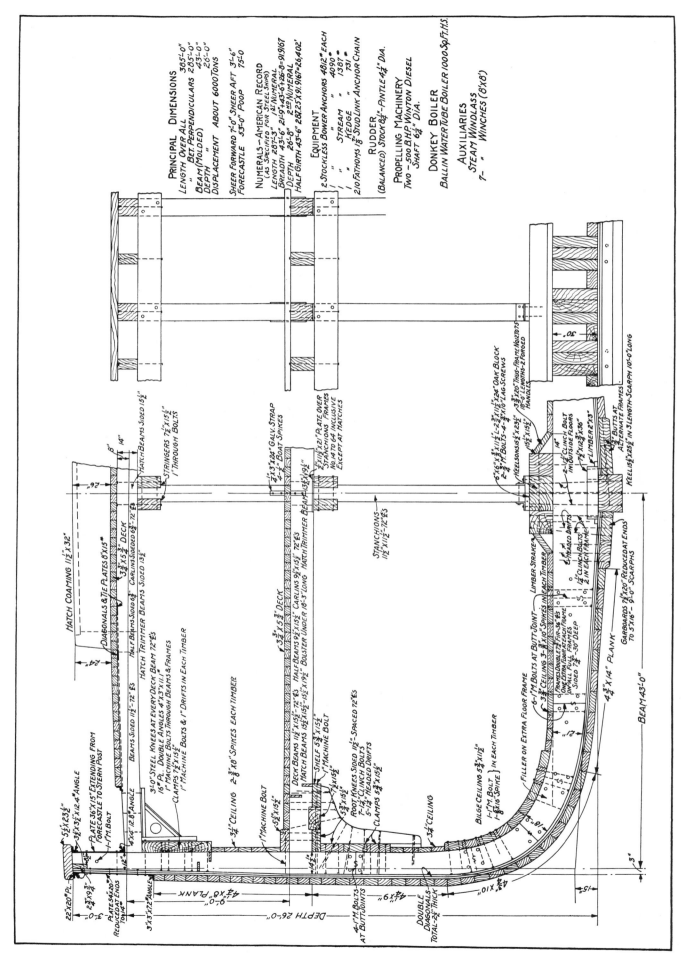

FIG. 40—MIDSHIP SECTION AND CONSTRUCTION DETAILS OF A 4000-TON MOTOR SHIP WITH DIAGONAL PLANKING

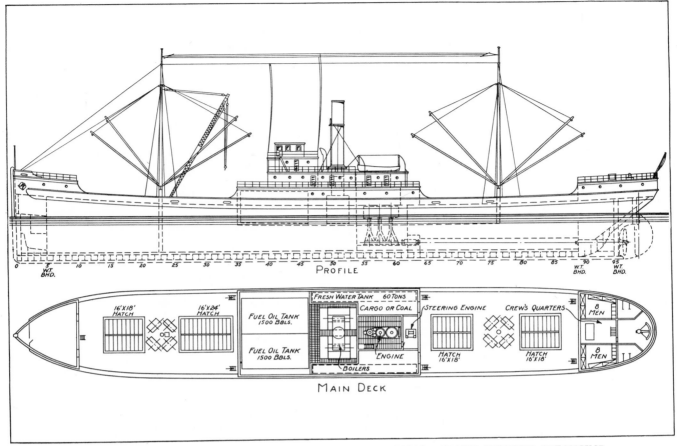

FIG. 41—OUTBOARD PROFILE AND DECK PLAN OF A TYPICAL 4000-TON WOODEN STEAMSHIP

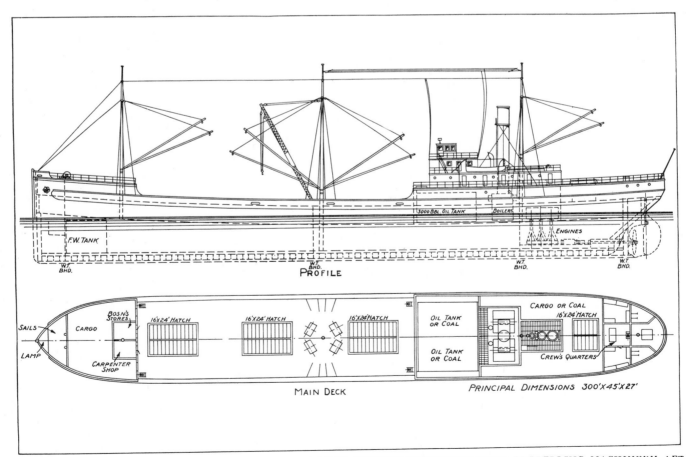

FIG. 42—OUTBOARD PROFILE AND DECK PLAN OF 4500-TON WOODEN STEAMSHIP WITH PROPELLING MACHINERY AFT

hold is obtained through three 16 x 24-foot hatches.

A full-powered, 4000-ton motor ship of the standard Pacific coast type is shown in Fig. 43. This vessel is equipped with twin screws, each driven by a 400-horsepower, 6-cylinder oil engine. The boat is 265 feet in length, 43 feet beam and 26 feet deep. The machinery is placed aft as in the case of the steam vessel shown in Fig. 42. The general arrangement of the hull in fact, is very similar to that of the steamer. The main hold is reached by three hatches, the forward one being 16 x 23 feet and the after two 16 x 26 feet. The cabin accommodations are ample and plenty of oil capacity has been provided. The three vessels shown in Figs. 41, 42 and 43 were designed by Fred A. Ballin, Portland, Oreg.

Fig. 36 shows the midship section of

keelson and by steel arch strapping on the sides.

The floors, which are sided 12 inches, are 26½ inches deep at the keel and 19 inches at the lower turn of the bilge. The frames, which also are sided 12 inches, are molded 16 inches at the upper turn of the bilge and 10 inches at the main deck. The frames, of course, are double and are spaced on 32-inch centers. The keel is 20 x 24 inches with a 4 x 20-inch false keel or shoe. The three garboard strakes on either side of the keel are 11 x 18, 9 x 18 and 7 x 16 inches, respectively. Between the garboard strakes and the bilge keels there are three courses of planking, 5 x 16 inches, 5 x 14 inches and 5 x 12 inches, respectively. The bilge keels, which are arranged as shown in Fig. 36, are 12 x 16 inches, fitted with a 4 x 12-inch shoe. Above the bilge keels there

of an arch, extending up to the height of the hold beams amidship and tapering down on both ends. The general arrangement of this central girder is shown clearly in Fig. 44.

The method of fastening the various elements of the hull structure together is shown clearly in Fig. 36.

The steel reinforcing consists of two arch straps on each side of the vessel. These straps, which are built up of ¾ x 14-inch universal plates securely riveted together at the ends, are let into the frames under the planking as shown in Fig. 36. The two lines of strapping are about eight feet apart. They extend the full length of the ship in the form of an arch rising amidship to a point 3 feet above the main deck. At the ends they run down to the line of the bilge. These straps, supplemented by the center girder-keelson, add considerably to

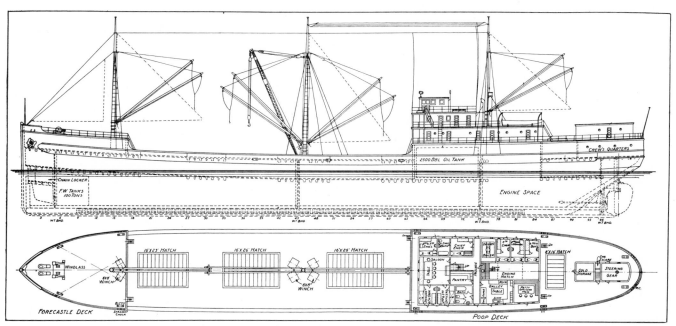

FIG. 43—OUTBOARD PROFILE AND DECK PLAN OF 4000-TON MOTOR SHIP DESIGNED FOR OVERSEAS SERVICE

the standard 5-masted auxiliary schooner illustrated in Figs. 35 and 44. A number of these vessels have been built by the Grays Harbor Ship Building Co., Grays Harbor, Wash. They are of the following dimensions: Length over all, 290 feet; length under deck, 274 feet; length between perpendiculars, 268 feet; beam, extreme, 48 feet; beam, molded, 46 feet, 10 inches; depth, molded, 26 feet 9 inches; depth of hold, 24 feet 6 inches. They are equipped with twin screws driven by 400-horsepower, 4-cylinder, crosshead type, 2-cycle oil engines built by the H. W. Sumner Co., Seattle.

A study of their cross section, Fig. 36, indicates that in their general design these vessels are similar to the standard Pacific coast type previously described, except that they are strengthened by means of a heavy center girder-

are two courses of planking consisting of eight strakes of 6 x 10-inch planks and 22 strakes of 7 x 8-inch planks.

The ceiling over the floors is 10 x 16 inches; over the bilges it is 14 x 14 inches and over the sides 12 x 12 inches. There are two sets of beams including 14 x 16-inch hold beams and 16 x 16-inch main beams. The hatch beams are 16 x 20 inches.

The keelson construction is one of the features of these vessels. The main keelson structure consists of five 20 x 20-inch pieces laid on the floors, surmounted by three 20 x 20-inch sister keelsons and a 20 x 24-inch rider. In addition, and this is where the construction differs from ordinary practice, there are eight 12 x 18-inch keelsons laid on top of the rider keelson. These latter keelsons form a sort of center girder. They are arranged in the shape

the longitudinal strength of the vessel. In addition, the deck beams are tied together by ¾ x 4-inch straps laid in four courses the full length of the ship. This vessel requires about 1,350,000 board feet of timber for its construction.

The cross section details of a 4000-ton wooden steamer are shown in Fig. 37. They form an interesting contrast to the motor ship illustrated in Fig. 36. This vessel is 290 feet in length over all, 270 feet between perpendiculars, 49 feet beam over the planking, with a depth of hold of 26 feet. In its general features, the design is somewhat similar to that prepared by Theodore E. Ferris for the United States Emergency Fleet Corp. The floors, however, have more dead rise than in the Ferris boat and some of the timber scantlings are different. The general dimensions of the planking and ceiling are about the

same as those in the motor ship shown in Fig. 36. A similar system of arch strapping also is employed. The straps extend for three-quarters the length of the vessel.

The keelson construction in this case consists of five 20 x 20-inch keelsons laid on the floors surmounted by three 20 x 20-inch sister keelsons and a 14 x 14-inch continuous rider. On either side of the rider are 6 x 14-inch stringers. Instead of the center girder-keelson illustrated in Fig. 36, a central longitudinal bulkhead is employed. It consists of stanchions at alternate beams connected by a bulkhead built up of 6 x 12-inch timbers. These timbers are further strengthened by 4 x 10-inch diagonals on both sides. The details of this bulkhead construction are clearly shown in Fig. 37.

The lower deck beams are sided 16 inches and molded 14 inches. They are spaced on 3-foot centers. The hatch end beams are sided 20 inches and molded 14 inches. The main deck beams are 16 inches x 14 inches. The

ings. Each hatch is divided into two parts by a filler consisting of two 14 x 16-inch pieces surmounted by a 14 x 20-inch continuous stringer. The overall dimensions of the hatches are 12 x 22 feet, except the forward hatch, which is 12 x 18 feet.

A Novel Design

Fig. 40 shows the cross section details of a 4000-ton motor ship designed by Fred A. Ballin, Supple & Ballin, Portland, Oreg. The construction adopted by Mr. Ballin presents several novel features, the object of the designer being to produce a boat which will have strength equivalent to that of a steel hull without using excessive amounts of timber. To accomplish this purpose, unusually deep floors are employed, together with a double diagonal inner skin of planking and specially designed steel topsides. The details of the design are shown clearly in Fig. 40. The boat, which has a displacement of about 6000 tons and a capacity of about 4000 tons is 308 feet in length over all

to the lower deck and 4¼ x 8 inches above that point. It will be understood, of course, that under this outer layer of ordinary planking are two thicknesses of 1¼-inch diagonal planking. This inner skin of double diagonals adds immensely to the strength of the hull. It also makes it possible to reduce the thickness of the ceiling very materially. Furthermore, the large number of keelsons commonly employed in Pacific coast ships are done away with. The keelsons in this vessel consist simply of one 15½ x 23½ inch main keelson with a 15½-inch square sister keelson on each side. The ceiling over the floor is 3¾ inches thick. The bilge ceiling is 5¾ x 11½ inches. The ceiling on the sides is 3¼ inches. The clamps under the lower deck beams are 5¾ x 15½ inches. Three are provided. Three 7½ x 15½-inch clamps likewise are provided under the main deck beams. The lower deck beams are braced by steel knees spaced on 72-inch centers. The upper deck beams are similarly supported by 3-foot steel knees also

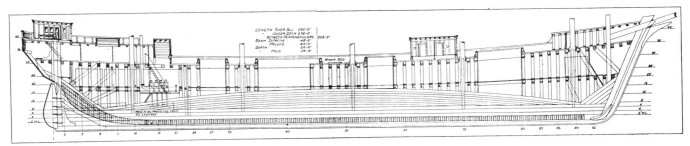

FIG. 44—INBOARD PROFILE OF 5-MASTED, TOPMAST AUXILIARY SCHOONER SHOWING ARRANGEMENT OF
CENTER GIRDER-KEELSON

frames which are spaced 36 inches are sided 12 inches and molded 26½ inches over the keel. They also are molded 19 inches at the lower turn of the bilge, 17 inches at the center of the bilge, 16 inches at the top of the bilge, 10 inches at the deck and 9 inches at the rail. The frames, of course, are double up to the rail, which is 6 x 30 inches in section.

It will be noted that the use of knees for holding the beams in place has been obviated by the employment of a clamp and shelf type of construction. The clamp consists of three 12 x 12-inch pieces surmounted by the shelf which is built up of 12 x 14-inch, 12 x 12-inch and 16 x 16-inch stringers as shown in Fig. 37. This shelf construction is used for supporting both the lower and upper deck beams.

Hatch Construction

The hatch construction also is interesting. On the lower deck it consists of a 16 x 18-inch trimmer surmounted by a 16 x 16-inch coaming. The upper deck hatches consist of 16 x 18-inch carlins surmounted by 16 x 18-inch continuous stringers and 16 x 16-inch coam-

and 285 feet between perpendiculars. The molded beam is 43 feet and the molded depth 26 feet. The sheer forward is 7 feet; aft, 3 feet 6 inches. This vessel is driven by two 500-horsepower 6-cylinder Winton engines, built by the Winton Gas Engine Works, Cleveland. These engines are connected to twin screws.

The frames, which it will be noted are spaced on 36-inch centers, are sided 7¾ inches and are molded as follows: 21 inches at the lower turn of the bilge, 18 inches at the middle of the bilge, 16½ inches at the upper turn of the bilge; 14½ inches at the lower deck and 12 inches at the upper deck. The floors, which also are sided 7¾ inches, are 30 inches deep over the keel. There is one extra floor at each frame on all full frames. The keel is 15½ x 25½ inches arranged in three lengths with 10-foot scarfs. On either side of the keel are two garboard strakes 7½ x 20 inches reduced at the ends to 5 x 16 inches. They are provided with 9-foot scarfs. Outside of the garboards the bottom planking is 4¾ x 14 inches. The outer bilge planking is 4¾ x 10 inches and the side planking is 4¼ x 9 inches

spaced on 72-inch centers. These knees are of plate and angle construction, their general arrangement being clearly indicated in Fig. 40.

This illustration also shows the details of the steel plate topside. This reinforcement consists of a 54-inch x 20-pound girder plate on the outside of the frames, a 36-inch x 15-pound girder plate on the inside of the frame and a 48-inch x 20-pound deck stringer plate. The two girder plates are tied together by a 22-inch x 20-pound rail plate, the connection being made 3½ x 3½ x 12.4 pound angles. The girder plates, also, are tied to the deck stringer plate by angles. The whole forms a very rigid topside construction, the details of which should be studied by referring to Fig. 40.

An Opinion From England

The merits of the double diagonal planking system adopted by Mr. Ballin, are interestingly set forth by W. H. White, late chief constructor of the royal navy, Great Britain, in his "Manual of Naval Architecture." In this book Mr. White says:

"Other composite ships have been con-

FIG. 45—A TYPICAL FOUR-MASTED WOODEN AUXILIARY SCHOONER UNDER CONSTRUCTION ON PUGET SOUND

structed with the skin planking in two thicknesses, one or both of which had the planks worked diagonally; it was then unnecessary to fit diagonal rider plates to assist the skin against racking strains.

The Diagonal System of Planking

"This diagonal system of planking has also been adopted in some special classes of wooden ships with great success. The royal yachts are examples of this system of construction. Three thicknesses of planking are employed, the two inside being worked diagonally and the outer one longitudinally. The two diagonal layers are inclined in opposite directions and the skin thus formed possesses such superior strength to the skin of an ordinary wooden ship that there need be comparatively little transverse framing above the bilges. Direct experiments with models and the experience gained with ships built on this plan, have demonstrated its great combination of strength and lightness. The royal yacht VICTORIA AND ALBERT, built on this plan, with her unusually powerful engines and high speed, is subjected to excessively great sagging moments, but has continued in service for nearly 40 years with complete exemption from signs of weakness. Like many other improved systems of construction, this is found rather more expensive than the common plan, but if wood had not been so largely superseded by iron and steel, probably much more extensive use would have been made of the diagonal system."

It is necessary when building a wooden ship to work out the weights of the various items in the structure carefully. The following table will give an idea of what these figures come to in the case of an actual ship. The figures given below are the hull weights of a motor schooner built by the Aberdeen Shipbuilding Co., Aberdeen, Wash., for the French-American Shipping Co., New York. These boats are 252 feet in length over all and 221 feet between perpendiculars. The length of the keel

is 220 feet. The extreme beam is 43 feet, the molded beam 40 feet 2 inches and the depth of hold is 21 feet. The hull weights are as follows:

Item	Pounds
Oakum	8,000
Auxiliaries	8,000
Anchors and chains	38,350
Boats	2,000
Cabin and forecastle fittings	10,000
Davits	2,000
Deck piping and pumps	3,000
Donkey boiler	8,000
Engine room piping, air bottles, lead sleeve	4,000
Exhaust piping	2,200
Fastenings	266,000
Fresh water	58,156
Lumber	3,166,350
Main engines	56,000
Oil	270,000
Propellers	4,000
Rigging	20,000
Spars	49,200
Shafting	10,000
Steering gear	1,000
Strut	4,000
Tanks	26,000
Windlass	16,000
Winches, 3	30,000
Spikes	40,000
Clinch rings	2,500
Iron bark	30,000
Paint	70,000
Total	4,206,756

An interesting formula for estimating the carrying capacity of wooden ships of the standard Pacific coast type with heavy center keelsons has been worked out by western engineers. This formula is as follows:

$C = 1.15 \ L \ W.$
Where C is the carrying capacity in pounds L is the number of board feet of lumber required to build ship.
W is the weight of the timber per board foot.

If actual experience is any guide, it requires from seven to nine months to build a wooden vessel on the Pacific coast under existing conditions. Claims have been made that 3500-ton boats could be built in four months, but in no case under the writer's observation, has this been substantiated, even approximately. It is the writer's judgment that with the proper yard organization and care in assembling materials promptly, these boats might be constructed in five or six months at the minimum.

While it is possible to crowd the construction by adding more men to the job, the point is soon reached where additional men do not result in propor-

tionately increased progress. One of the oldest practical ship builders on the Pacific coast claims that it is not economical to work over 50 to 60 men on one hull. About 25 per cent of these men should be skilled.

It is believed a study of the drawings, reproductions of photographs and data included in this chapter will give the reader a clear idea of the general features of modern wooden ship construction. It is not intended in this series to go into the theoretical side of the problem. The purpose of this work is simply to present practical facts regarding actual construction operations.

Theory is Complicated

If the reader is interested in becoming familiar with the methods of designing and laying down ships, including the preparation of the lines, the calculation of the displacements, trim, etc., he should refer to standard works on naval architecture dealing with this subject. It might be stated, however, that the theoretical side of ship design is exceedingly complicated. Even the comparatively simple problem of preparing the sheer draft or lines of a wooden vessel involves a knowledge of the principles of descriptive geometry not possessed by persons who have not made a special study of this branch of mathematics.

One great trouble, however, with the product of many modern wooden ship building yards, lies in the fact that in a large number of cases the boats are not designed by competent architects, but are simply built by rule of thumb methods. In this day and age, such procedure is hardly acceptable in any department of the mechanical world. On the other hand, it must be thoroughly understood that the scientific principles of ship designing cannot be learned in a few months, particularly by persons who have not had the benefit of general technical and mathematical training.

CHAPTER V

Details of Frame and Keel Construction

WE NOW come to the consideration of construction procedure, to the details of which the remaining chapters of this book will be devoted. Laying the keel is popularly supposed to be the first step in the construction of any vessel, be it wood or steel. As a matter of fact, it is not the first operation to be performed. Before the keel can be laid, the ways must be prepared and the keel blocks assembled in their proper position. The first step, therefore, in actually building a wooden ship, consists in preparing the ways or foundation. for the keel blocks. In European shipyards, the building slips or ways frequently are paved with stone in order to insure a permanently smooth, true surface. In such cases large blocks of wood are let into the masonry and the keel blocks, shores, etc., where necessary, are bolted or spiked to these blocks.

In American yards it is not considered necessary to pave the building slips. In fact, in most wooden shipyards, the amount of work involved in preparing the ways is comparatively slight. If solid ground is available on which the blocks may be laid, it is simply necessary to grade the site to a comparatively true surface. It is, of course, better in such cases if the ground slopes properly. If the ground has no slope it is necessary to build the blocks up rather high under the forward end of the vessel in order to give the proper declivity to the launching ways.

If the ground is sufficiently solid, the keel blocks can be laid directly on the earth, which in some cases may be tamped a trifle. If the ground is soft or if it has been recently filled, piles must be driven to support the weight of the ship under construction. In some cases, particularly on the Pacific coast, as previously mentioned, the entire building slip rests on piles which may be driven out over the water to a considerable distance. In cases where this is done in salt water, more or less frequent repairs will have to be made to the foundation. It is better, therefore, where possible, to lay the keel blocks on dry land.

Arrangement of Keel Blocks

The keel blocks usually are arranged as shown in Figs. 53 and 54. The structure, it will be noted from these illustrations, consists simply of blocks about 16 inches square and 6 to 8 feet in length, piled between 2 x 12-inch planks which run parallel to the keel. From two to three planks are placed between each layer of blocks. The planks give the structure what little longitudinal stability it needs.

The blocks are laid to the proper declivity by stretching a cord between fixed points, the correct height of which have been determined either by direct measurement or means of a civil engineer's level. Most authorities state that the keel blocks should be laid to a declivity of ⅝ inch per foot. On the Pacific coast, in most cases it has been found this is not enough to get the vessel properly started down the ways. In one case it took 20 men half a day to get the ship started after the launching should have taken place. Most western ship builders today are laying their blocks to a grade of ¾ inch or 1 inch per foot.

It should be remembered that when the ship is launched her after part is raised by the bouyancy of the water and if proper care is not taken in arranging the declivity of the keel blocks, the forefoot may touch the ground when the ship has reached the end of the ways. In some cases, to prevent this it has been found necessary to excavate or dredge the lower end of the slip after the vessel is finished.

In preparing the building slip, therefore, there are three important considerations to be kept in mind. They are as follows:

1.—To provide sufficient space between the ship and the ground for performing all the building operations at the keel and bilges.
2.—To leave sufficient space between the ground and bilges, and one-sixth the breadth of the ship at each side of the keel for fitting the ground ways, and for driving in the wedges which tighten the cradle under the ship, so as to support her after the shores and blocks are knocked away.

FIG. 46—FRAME OF A TYPICAL WOODEN VESSEL NEARLY READY FOR PLANKING

FIG. 47—LAYING-DOWN THE LINES OF A SHIP ON THE MOLD-LOFT FLOOR

FIG. 48—LAYING THE KEEL OF A 4000-TON MOTOR SHIP

FIG. 49—FINISHING THE FRAMING OF A LARGE WOODEN SHIP ON THE PACIFIC COAST

3.—To make such an allowance for the excess, if any, in the declivity of the launching ways over that of the blocks as will prevent the forefoot of the ship from touching the ground when she has reached the end of the ways, as previously explained.

In order to obtain the required height of the foremost block with great accuracy a sketch of the ground or slip upon which the ship is to be built should be made in elevation and section, and two pieces of cardboard should be cut, one to the shape of the transverse and the other to the longitudinal section of the ship, both drawings and cardboards being on the same scale. By placing the cards on the sketches and trying them in various positions, all risk of error in deciding the height of the foremost block can be avoided.

The launching ways usually are set at a greater declivity than the keel blocks and the amount that the forefoot of the ship falls below the line of the blocks when it reaches the lowest part of the slip can be found by a simple mathematical calculation. Clearance between the forefoot and the ground should not be less than 9 to 12 inches. Now in the case of a ship built on a slip 300 feet long, on blocks at an inclination of ⅝ inch to a foot, and launched at ¾ inch to a foot, it is evident that the bow falls ⅛ inch below the line of the blocks for every foot the ship slides down the ways. Hence, in the 300 feet, there is a total relative fall of 37½ inches, and therefore, the foremost block, if at the head of the slip, must be kept 37½ inches plus 12 inches, or 49½ inches above a line,

FIG. 50—FRAMING STAGE LAID ALONGSIDE KEEL—THE FRAMES ARE HOISTED INTO POSITION BY MEANS OF A SIMPLE TACKLE

which, at an inclination of ⅝ inch to the foot just touches the after end of the ship.

From these data the foremost block can be readily built to its correct height. In order to lay the other blocks, instead of using the string or cord previously mentioned, a declivity batten may be prepared. This is a batten about 20 feet long, the edges of which are straight and inclined to each other at an angle equal to the required declivity of the blocks. Now put up a block at 20 feet abaft the foremost one to such a height as will cause the upper edge of the batten to be level, as indicated by a spirit level, while the lower edge rests upon the two blocks. These two blocks will now have the proper declivity with reference to each other.

The other blocks are laid in a similar manner, or by sighting them with the two first placed, and when this is done they can all be proved by stretching a

line along their upper surfaces or by trying the declivity batten along the whole range of blocks.

After the blocks are laid out, in some yards they are secured to the ground by nails, dogs, etc., and if necessary, to each other. Spur shores also are recommended, reaching from the foreside of each block near the ground to the upper part of the after side of the one in front of it, in order to prevent the blocks from tripping, a casualty which has at times occurred when such precautions have not been taken.

The keel rests on short blocks about 10 inches thick which are supported on wedges as shown in Fig. 55. These wedges serve a double purpose. They make it easy to bring the blocks exactly up to the line so that each pier supports its proper proportion of the weight and in addition, when the ship is to be launched they may be readily knocked out of position with a sledge.

FIG. 51—ASSEMBLING FRAME FUTTOCKS ON FRAMING STAGE

FIG. 52—RESAWING FRAME JOINTS TO A PROPER FIT

FIG. 53—SETTING KEEL BLOCKS TO THE PROPER HEIGHT FIG. 54—SETTING KEEL BLOCKS ON SAND FIG. 55—KEEL WEDGED IN PLACE ON KEEL BLOCKS FIG. 56—LAYING THE KEEL IN A SOUTHERN SHIPYARD FIG. 57 SCAFFOLDING ARRANGED ALONGSIDE KEEL BLOCKS FIG. 58—KEEL NEAR STERN

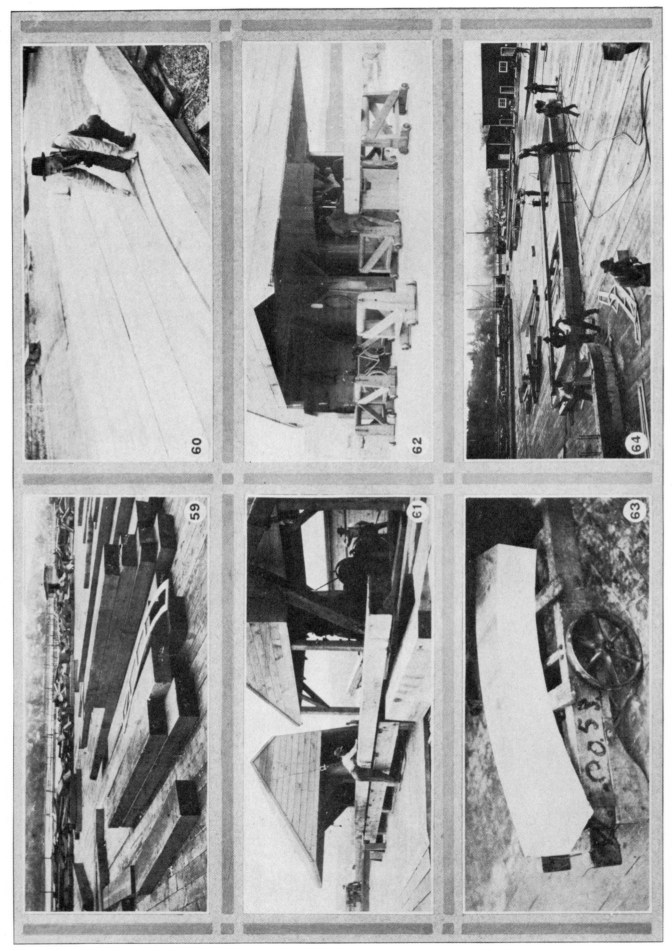

FIG. 59—FRAME TIMBERS AND MOLDS FIG. 60—MARKING FRAME TIMBERS FIG. 61—CUT-OFF SAW FOR FRAME TIMBERS FIG. 62—BAND SAW FOR SHAPING FRAME TIMBERS FIG. 63—A FRAME FUTTOCK AFTER LEAVING THE BAND SAW FIG. 64—GENERAL ARRANGEMENT OF FRAMING STAGE

FIG. 65—SETTING FRAMES BY MEANS OF A TRAVELING CRANE

at the scarf. The joints of the scarf frequently are laid in carbolineum to prevent decay and also to resist the action of the sea animalculæ. As soon as the keel is laid, its alignment is secured against disturbance by means of sway braces spaced every 30 or 40 feet, as shown in Figs. 55 and 56. The brace used in Fig. 55 is 6 inches square.

After the keel pieces are laid on the blocks and fitted together, the whole is sighted and proved to be straight. When this is accomplished, the keel is secured in the correct position by driving short treenails in the blocks close against the side of the keel. All of the bolts are now driven through the keel scarfs. The positions of the frame stations are next transferred to the keel, after which it is ready to receive the frames and to be joined to the stem and stern posts.

In order to prevent any water which may find its way into the joints of the

After the site is prepared, the work of arranging the keel blocks and the preparations for laying the keel should take less than a week. The actual laying of the keel for a 300-foot boat can be accomplished in a day or two. In some yards, the blocks are piled up crib fashion as shown in Fig. 56, which illustrates the method employed in a wooden shipyard in Georgia.

Getting Out the Keel

The keel is made of long pieces of selected timber similar to that shown in Fig. 48. On the Pacific coast these pieces can easily be obtained in lengths up to 100 feet. These extra long lengths, of course, reduce the number of joints or scarfs. In order to preserve their continuity as much as possible, the various sections of the keel are scarfed together as shown in Fig. 55. These scarfs may be from 10 to 20 feet in length. The two pieces, of course, are thoroughly bolted together

FIG. 67—FRAMES RAISED, READY FOR PLUMBING AND HORNING

keel scarfs from getting behind the garboards, a stopwater may be placed in the joint of the scarf. This stopwater consists simply of a plug of soft pine driven tightly into a hole bored right through the joint. The expansion of the plug, when immersed, prevents water from going up through the scarf and getting behind the bottom planking.

We now take up the question of preparing the frames and placing them in their proper positions on the keel. The framing is one of the most important parts of the ship's structure, which consists, essentially of nothing more than a series of transverse ribs covered with a longitudinal series of planks which bind the frames together and keep out the water. The frames usually are spaced at equidistant intervals, the length of which is known as a "room and space." The length of the room and space is fixed by the designer. On

FIG. 66—RAISING FRAMES BY MEANS OF BLOCK AND TACKLE

FIG. 68—HAND-WINCH FOR HAULING TIMBERS THROUGH BAND SAW   FIG. 69—DETAIL OF BOLTED FRAME JOINTS
FIG. 70—ANOTHER VIEW OF BOLTED FRAME CONSTRUCTION   FIG. 71—RIBBANDS IN PLACE AND SHORING
UNDER FRAME

FIG. 72—FRAMING STAGE IN A GEORGIA SHIPYARD

FIG. 73—FRAME OF A VESSEL IN A GEORGIA SHIPYARD

FIG. 74—TWO SETS OF CROSS SPALLS SOMETIMES ARE USED TO HOLD THE FRAME SECTIONS TOGETHER

FIG. 75—UPPER PART OF ARCH STRAPPING

account of the great curvature of the transverse sections of the vessel, especially amidships, it is necessary to build the frames of a number of pieces and in order that these may be united as rigidly as possible, they are disposed in two sets, the butts of which give shift to each other, the whole being so combined that its elements will yield mutual support in the most efficient manner obtainable.

Preparing the Molds

The proper curves or molds for the frame sections are provided by the mold loft, where the sheer-draft or lines of the vessel are laid down full size. Fig. 47 shows a view of a mold loft, indicating how the lines are laid down for the preparation of the molds. The mold loft should be big enough so the longitudinal or sheer-plan of the vessel can be laid down in at least two sections. In many cases, however, it is necessary to lay down the ship in three sections.

A sheer-draft, as the lines of the vessel frequently are called, usually is prepared in the drawing room to a scale of ¼ inch to the foot. When this is copied to full size on the mold-loft floor, it may be found that errors, almost inappreciable in the quarter scale drawings are very apparent when magnified 48 times. It is usually found, therefore, that the three sets of lines, namely, the sheer-plan, body-plan, and half-breadth plan, disagree sufficiently to prevent the various problems of laying off from being solved with that degree of accuracy which is necessary in order to obtain a fair surface to the vessel. Hence a fairing or correcting process has to be performed before the molds can be prepared.

As every draftsman knows, the projections of the lines of the vessel upon the three plans, sheer, body and half-breadth, are mutually interdependent and this property is utilized in performing the fairing operation. The projections of each of the sets of lines used in this process, that is the water-lines or level lines, cross sections or square sections, bow lines and diagonal lines, appear straight in one or two of the three plans, so that by the aid of a straightedge they can be drawn fair easily in such plans. Now the property which a wooden or metallic batten has of bending in a fair curve is brought into play in drawing the lines fairly in the plans where they appeared curved. Since the intersections of lines with each other are points, the points of intersection of two sets of lines in one plan are transferred to their relative positions in the others, so that points which appear straight in one plan form a curved line in another. Battens are penned or bent to pass through as many of the points as is consistent with absolute fairness and the line is drawn. Thus, by a series of interchanges between the three plans, or projections of the lines, the various lines are copied from one plan into another

until at length all the plans coincide and the lines composing them are continuous curves. The fact that the curves are continuous proves that the body is fair.

It is a great advantage if the seams of the boards forming the floor of the mold loft are perfectly straight and parallel, as they thus afford considerable assistance in the several processes of squaring and drawing parallel lines which are involved in the practice of laying-off.

Transferring Lines to the Floor

The first thing to be done in copying the lines onto the mold loft floor is to strike a base-line. If the edges of the boards are arranged as suggested, it will be necessary to place the base-line either parallel or perpendicular to the lines of seams. Should the floor be rectangular, about two feet from the wall or other boundary of the floor is a convenient position for a base-line. After the base-line is drawn, the depth of the keel, the lower edge of planking, and the upper side of the keel are set off from it at distances measured from the sheer-plan. Also the fore and after-edges of the stem together with the fore-edge of rabbet of stem, which is, of course, a continuation of the lower edge of planking on the keel, are laid off. The sternpost is next copied with the after-edge of its rabbet and the various square stations, or frame stations in the sheer-plan are laid out on the floor. These, with the line of the upper deck beams at the middle, are termed the fixed lines of the sheer-plan, being unalterable except insofar as drawing them true is concerned.

To economize space, the half-breadth plan is generally drawn on the same part of the mold loft floor as the sheer-plan. The base-line of the former, or a line parallel thereto serving as the middle

FIG. 76—LOWER PART OF ARCH STRAPPING SHOWING METHOD OF FASTENING THE BUTTS

FIG. 77—DETAIL OF STANDARD FRAME CONSTRUCTION   FIG. 78—DETAIL OF BOLTED FRAME CONSTRUCTION   FIG. 79-
FRAME NEAR BOW USING NATURAL CROOKS   FIG. 80—FRAMING A SHIP IN A SOUTHERN YARD   FIG. 81—
SOMETIMES THE FLOORS ARE LAID FIRST AND THE SIDE FRAME PIECES RAISED AFTERWARD
FIG. 82—DETAIL OF FRAMES HEELING TO DEADWOOD

line of the latter, and in this way the same square stations will do for the two plans.

Now, having copied the sheer-plan, the body-plan is next copied full size as nearly as possibly to the sheer-plan. In some cases where the mold loft floor is smaller than it should be, two plans overlap. On a very small floor, the same base-line may as well serve for three plans, one of the square stations in the midship being taken as the middle line of the body-plan.

Copying the Body Plan

The body-plan is copied or drawn on the floor by measuring the distances along the several water and diagonal lines from the middle line to where they cut the square stations, setting these distances off to full size on the corresponding lines on the floor. Battens are then penned or bent as in Fig. 47 so as to approximate as closely to these points as is consistent with absolute fairness or continuity. The lines then are marked in, usually with thin slices of chalk. At some yards it is customary to measure the ordinates, etc., and record them on paper in tabulated form before proceeding to draw the body full size on the floor. In this case, the latter operation is performed without direct reference to the drawing when working on the floor.

The half-breadth plan is next to be drawn on the floor and here we again note that the lines which are curved in the body plan are straight in the half-breadth plan and *vice versa*.

Having already drawn the middle line of the half-breadth plan on the floor and the projections of the square stations in that plan, we proceed to copy the level or water lines from the body plan into the half-breadth plan. For this purpose straightedged battens are set to the middle lines of the body and half-breadth plans on the drawings. Now measure on a staff whose end is kept against the batten set to the middle line of the body-plan, the distance from this line to where a level line cuts each square station or frame station in the body-plan. Transfer these distances to the corresponding square stations in the half-breadth plan on the floor by setting the end of the staff against the middle-line batten of that plan, marking the distances out from the respective square stations. A batten is then bent so it can pass fairly through as many as possible of these points, thus transferring the water lines to the half-breadth plan.

The diagonal lines and bow and buttock lines from the sheer-draft are also transferred full size to the mold loft floor in much the same manner as just described. In fact, this process of transferring the lines to the floor is comparatively simple if the principles of projection which underlie all drafting work are thoroughly understood. To be completely successful, the mold loft man also should have a good knowledge of descriptive geometry, which covers the details of the science of projection.

As the various plans are copied on the floor it is found that there are discrepancies, as previously pointed out. These must be corrected by mutual adjustment until the three plans coincide accurately.

When discrepancies occur, the water and diagonal lines in the neighborhood must be examined to see if the points within the section were correctly taken, and if a modification of these lines, consistent with fairness, will give such points as the batten will spring to. The bow and buttock lines are a great help to both the designer and the draftsman in judging the character of the surface at the extremities of the ship. No rules, however, can be laid down for guidance in dealing with them, experience being required in order that they may afford a vivid conception of the form of the vessel.

In practically performing all of the operations connected with laying down the lines on the mold loft floor, a great deal must be left to the judgment of the man in charge. A practiced eye will save much labor. When a batten does not spring well to the point, it is bent to pass outside some and inside others. As a rule the batten should pass on the outside more frequently than on the inside of the points in order that the volume of the ship may not be less than that given by the design. In copying and drawing the body-plan, it is advisable to draw the midship section first and then the others in rotation as the draftsman is thus better enabled to see what he is doing and exercise his judgment.

Time Required for Framing

Mold loft floors usually are painted. Generally a gray color is chosen. When a new set of lines is to be laid down, it usually is advisable to repaint the floor in order to completely obliterate all of the old lines. In some cases, however, the floors are not painted, but are left in a natural color. In these yards when new lines are to be laid down, the whole floor is gone over with a cabinet scraper, thus removing the old drawing. The finished molds are similar to those shown on the pile of timber in Fig. 59. White pine, cedar, or other easily worked strips are used for making molds.

As soon as the molds are ready, the process of framing the ship actually may be begun. This process may be divided into three steps as follows:

Sawing the frame sections; assembling the sections, or futtocks; and raising the frame.

The time required to frame a ship seems to vary widely in different yards. In one case the writer has been informed that 46 days were required to frame a 250-foot, 4-masted schooner. In this yard the frames were skidded into position and raised by tackle, no cranes being available. In another yard only 15 days were required to frame the square body of a 290-foot ship, using the same method of raising the frames. To this should be added 10 days for the forward and stern cant frames. A gang of about eight to 10 men is required, not including those working on the framing stage where a dozen more are necessary. After the main frames are up the smaller pieces of the stern frame, including the transom, etc., can be framed with a gang of four or five men.

Specifications of Timber Needed

The frames of modern wooden vessels are sawed from timbers similar to those shown in Fig. 59. The sizes of timbers necessary and the quantity required for framing a 300-foot vessel are indicated by the following quotation from the timber schedule for standard Pacific coast type wooden steamship, designed by Mr. Ferris for the United States Emergency Fleet Corp. The standard government boat, it will be recalled is 281 feet 6 inches in length overall and 46 feet beam. It has a cargo capacity of about 3500 tons on a draft of 23½ feet. The frame timber specifications are as follows:

Net size	Gross size	Length	No. of pieces	Feet B. M.
12 x 32	12¼ x 32	10	100	32,667
12 x 30	12¼ x 30	10	16	4,900
12 x 30	12¼ x 30	10	100	30,625
12 x 30	12¼ x 30	16	12	5,880
12 x 30	12¼ x 30	20	16	9,800
12 x 30	12¼ x 30	24	12	8,820
12 x 28	12¼ x 28	12	16	5,488
12 x 28	12¼ x 28	16	50	22,867
12 x 28	12¼ x 28	16	56	25,611
12 x 26	12¼ x 26	10	100	26,541
12 x 26	12¼ x 26	16	56	23,781
12 x 26	12¼ x 26	16	50	21,233
12 x 26	12¼ x 26	28	20	14,863
12 x 26	12¼ x 26	28	16	11,891
12 x 26	12¼ x 26	30	80	63,700
12 x 24	12¼ x 24	16	56	21,952
12 x 24	12¼ x 24	16	50	19,600
12 x 24	12¼ x 24	16*	5	2,940
12 x 20	12¼ x 20	12	50	12,250
12 x 20	12¼ x 20	16	56	18,293
12 x 16	12¼ x 16	12	56	10,976
12 x 16	12¼ x 16	12	50	9,800
12 x 16	12¼ x 16	14	80	18,293
12 x 12	12¼ x 12	16	80	15,680
10 x 24	10¼ x 24	16*	5	2,400

*And up, average 24 feet.

It also may be interesting to note that the timber required for frames Nos. 35 to 60 in the 5-masted motorschooner, the details of which were presented in Figs. 36 and 44, in the fourth chapter of this book, pages 24 and 30, are as follows:

13 pieces................ 12 x 28 — 40
13 pieces................ 12 x 20 — 30
39 pieces................ 12 x 26 — 32

13 pieces................. 12 x 22 — 22
13 pieces................. 12 x 25 — 34
20 pieces................. 12 x 22 — 36
16 pieces................. 12 x 18 — 40
10 pieces................. 12 x 18 — 42

Forward Cant Frame No. 92

1 piece................... 12 x 26 — 24
1 piece................... 12 x 28 — 36
1 piece................... 12 x 24 — 22
1 piece................... 12 x 20 — 28
1 piece................... 12 x 28 — 24
1 piece................... 12 x 16 — 28

One method of marking the frame timbers with the molds is shown clearly in Fig. 60. A man of some experience is necessary for this operation and a good workman can save considerable lumber at this point. After the frame timbers have been properly marked, they are ready to be sawed and for this purpose sawing equipment such as that illustrated in Figs. 61 and 62 may be employed. The equipment shown in Fig. 61 consists of a 48-inch swinging cut-off saw and a steam-driven derrick with a 45-foot boom. As soon as the timbers are marked, as shown in Fig. 60, they are picked up by the derrick and swung around to the cut-off saw table as indicated in Fig. 61. After being sawed to the proper length, they are skidded out onto the horses shown at the extreme left in the background in Fig. 61. They are then transferred from the horses to dollies or timber trucks similar to those shown in Fig. 62. These dollies are used to shift the timbers to the band-saw.

Roughing Out the Timber

A 40-inch bandsaw is provided. The frames are sawed to the proper curved outlines in the band-saw, the finished sections or futtocks appearing as in Fig. 63. This also shows the type of truck used for transferring the finished frame sections from the band-saw to the framing stage where the frames are assembled. In some yards, in order to assist the work of sawing, small hand winches, such as that shown in Fig. 68, are employed. This apparatus saves considerable labor. It is particularly useful in sawing bevels on long straight pieces. For sawing out the frames of a 300-foot vessel, a gang of seven to nine men, using the equipment just described, is employed. It takes such a gang about nine weeks to saw out the 100 frames in the ship. If the gang turns out four complete single frames in an 8-hour shift, a good day's work has been accomplished. If greater speed is desired, more men and equipment must be employed.

After the frame sections are sawed out, they must be assembled. This operation is shown in Figs. 51, 52 and 64. The framing stage of a southern shipyard also is shown in Fig. 72. The framing stage, on which the various sections are assembled, is located usually at the head of the building slip. Sometimes, as in Fig. 50, it is built

right alongside the keel so that the assembled frames do not have to be moved before they are rolled up into place. Preferably, however, the framing stage should be level. At all events it should have a plane surface. As shown in Fig. 51, wedges are used to bring the various sections or futtocks to proper alignment. The joints, it will be noted, do not fit exactly. They, therefore, are resawed using cross-cut saws as shown in Fig. 52. This illustration shows the frame after the doubling frame is in place. The several futtocks must be fastened together before the frame is hoisted into place. Usually wooden treenails, such as those shown at the left in Fig. 64, are utilized for this purpose. The tops of the frames also are tied together by means of cross spalls. Single pieces of 2 x 6-inch timber usually are employed for this purpose.

After the frame has been assembled as shown in Fig. 64 it must be raised into position. Various methods are employed. Perhaps the most rapid and efficient is that illustrated in Fig. 65, using the traveling derrick described in Chapter III, and described in detail on page 22.

As this illustration indicates, the derrick readily picks up the frame and takes it down to its proper position on the keel. The derrick also is of advantage in the plumbing and horning operations. As soon as the frame is secured in place, it is fastened to its neighbor by means of light tie pieces and small bolts as shown in Fig. 50. Groups of frames when they are erected, are later tied together by ribbands as shown in Figs. 71 and 78. The derrick shown in Fig. 65 is at the plant of the Sloan Shipyards Corp., Olympia, Wash.

When the services of a derrick or crane are not available, the simpler method of rolling the frame into position by means of tackle as shown in Fig. 66 may be employed. This method of raising frames is employed in the yard shown in Fig. 50. This illustration shows clearly how the frame is hoisted into position using tackle fastened to the upper ends of frames already raised.

Southern Practice

A good view of a set of frames after hoisting is shown in Fig. 74. This illustrates the practice of a Georgia yard. It will be noted that two sets of ties are used to hold the frames together. Another view of the frame construction of a wooden motor schooner built in the same yard is shown in Fig. 79. This shows how natural crooks are employed to strengthen the frame members near the bow. It must be admitted that these frames are stronger than those which

are merely sawed out. There is not, however, enough timber of suitable character available to permit any large number of ships being built in this country in the manner shown in Fig. 79.

Detailed views of modern methods of fastening sawed frame futtocks together are shown in Figs, 69, 70, 77, and 78. The standard Pacific coast and Gulf construction is shown in Fig. 77. These frames are sawed out as previously described and as the illustration just mentioned indicates, the futtocks are fastened together by wooden treenails and drift bolts. Other shipbuilders, notably Fred A. Ballin, Portland, Oreg., use the bolted construction illustrated in Figs. 69, 70, and 78. Two bolts are carried through each end of the futtock forming a solid joint.

Further Construction Details

Further details of methods of shoring up frames after they are erected may be obtained from a study of Fig. 71. These shores are 6 inches square and it will be noted they are wedged to a bearing. The ribbands which hold the frames together temporarily are about 4 inches square and are spiked once to each frame. They are, of course, removed when the planking goes on. Wedges driven by hand mauls usually are employed for this purpose. In some cases, 6 x 6-inch ribbands are used. As a matter of fact, their exact dimensions are of no consequence. Neither is it necessary that they follow the diagonal lines as some old-line shipbuilders stipulate. Their sole purpose is simply to hold the frames together temporarily.

In setting frames, it is customary to start at the after end of the boat as shown in Fig. 65. Sometimes, however, the after cant frames are omitted, the square body being framed up first. In other yards, particularly in the south, the floors are first laid, and some of the keelsons bolted down, after which the side futtocks of the frames are set in place as shown in Fig. 81.

The frames, of course, cannot be secured by ribbands until the builder is sure they are set square with the keel and with each other. The following method may be employed to determine whether or not the frame is vertically square to the keel. Drop a plumb from the middle of the cross spall to the floor. Then measure the thickness of the cross spall from the joint of the frame, and set off this distance from the joint on the floor. The plumb should fall as much abaft this point as is given by the product of the declivity of the keel blocks per foot by the number of feet in the height of the cross spall above the floor. Of course, this is on the supposition that the frames are to be square to the keel which is true al-

most universally at the present time. In some old ships the frames are square to the load waterline instead of to the keel. In such cases, the necessary allowance must be made.

To determine whether or not the frame is horizontally square to the keel, the following procedure may be adopted: A point is selected on the middle line of the keel at some distance from the frame to be horned, as it is termed, and two other points are marked at equal heights on each side of the frame, say at a frame head. The distance from these latter points to the point on the middle line of keel will be equal if the frame is horizontally square to the keel. It is not necessary to horn every frame in this way nor to check its vertical inclination, since by the aid of ribband battens, when one frame is set correctly a number of others can be set by reference to it. It is, however, advisable to institute checks at intervals. The breadth of the ship at the different frame heads also should be checked from time to time, so that by plumbing and horning, the frames of the ship can be so shored and secured as to insure her external surface being of the designed form.

Putting on Arch Straps

The general method of reinforcing the frames of a wooden ship with steel strapping have been discussed in a previous chapter. When arch strapping, using 14-inch universal plates of the type shown in Figs. 75 and 76 is employed, the frames must be mortised out properly to let in the straps, so the planks will rest on a fair surface. The method of doing this is clearly indicated in Fig. 76, which also shows how the butts of the straps are fastened together and how the straps are bolted to the frames. The upper part of the steel arch where it rises to a point above the main deck is shown in Fig. 75. This form of strapping costs about $3000, including about $1500 for labor and fastenings.

Near the stern of the ship, the frames must be carefully heeled to the deadwood. Fig. 82 shows how this is done. It also shows how the deadwood is clamped together by means of chains and wedges before it is edgebolted.

FIG. 83—BOW CONSTRUCTION OF A LARGE PACIFIC COAST MOTOR SCHOONER

CHAPTER VI

Methods of Framing Forward End of Ship

IN FRAMING the ends of a ship special problems are encountered. The stem, at the forward end and the sternpost at the rear, must be set in place and the surrounding timbers properly arranged before the planking operations can be commenced. Of the two ends of the vessel, the framing of the bow is much the simpler.

Today wooden ships usually are built with either clipper bows or steamer bows. Vessels with auxiliary power usually are provided with clipper bows while full-powered motor vessels or steamships have steamer bows with the customary straight stem. The chief characteristics of these two types of bows are generally understood. The steamer bow is perhaps the less artistic of the two, although easier to frame. In the steamer bow the stem is set perpendicular to the keel; in the clipper type bow, the stem has a rake forward and is set at an acute angle to the keel. A typical clipper bow, with the framing in place ready for planking, is shown in Fig. 83. A steamer bow, in a similar stage of completion is shown in Fig. 94.

The bow construction of modern wooden ships has been greatly simplified by the large timbers now available in all sections of the United States, particularly on the Pacific coast. In the old days in England it was necessary to build up the stem. deadwood, apron, knighthead. etc., out of a great many pieces, all of which had to be carefully locked. scarfed, hooked and bolted together. In some old English ships of the line, as many as 34 pieces were used in the stem construction. The stem proper of modern wooden ships can be easily fashioned from one piece. The apron likewise can be made of one piece, and the knightheads may be similarly gotten out. As shown in Figs. 84

and 96, the frames near the stem must be swung or canted forward, out of square with the line of the keel. This is done in order to avoid excessive molding dimensions. Frames which are so swung are termed cant frames, whether they are located in the forward or after part of the vessel. The remaining frames, usually, are known as square frames. On the Pacific coast at the present time, however, the term cant frame is more loosely construed to mean any frame which heels against the deadwood as in Fig. 96, instead of against the keel.

On account of the tapering of the ship toward the forward end. it is necessary to fill up the thin portion with blocks of timber termed deadwood in order to form a suitable footing for the frames. In the case of clipper type ships, such as that shown in Fig. 83, it is not possible, even, to heel all of the frames against the deadwood, and some of the shorter ones near the upper part of the stem are heeled against the apron, which is a piece fitted immediately behind the stem. This construction is clearly shown in Figs. 83 and 89. The short timbers in the latter illustration, parallel to the stem, are known as knightheads. They are utilized to fill out the framing where the bows are comparatively blunt. Some years ago

old-line English wooden shipbuilders thought it absolutely necessary to use oak for the stems of wooden ships. Modern experience, has indicated, however, that this is not necessary at all, and at the present time fir, yellow pine and other woods are employed with equal success. In fact, the latter woods are preferable on account of the large sizes in which the timbers may be obtained. The advantage of using larger timbers already has been discussed.

If, however, it is necessary to build up the stem of more than one piece, the sections should be connected by scarfs similar to those used to connect the pieces of keel together. These scarfs should be so disposed as to give a good shift to the pieces of the apron, in case the latter also is composed of more than one piece. On account of the strain to which they are subjected, it is not a bad idea to dowel scarfs of this character.

Prior to 1850 it was customary to join the stem to the fore piece of keel by means of a curved scarf. It was necessary, therefore, to convert the stem from a timber which already had the necessary natural curvature so as to avoid shortness of grain at the thin lip of the scarf. In such cases. also, to aid in the conversion of the timbers, a portion of the curvature of the fore-foot was included in the fore-piece of keel by placing the scarf a little higher up the stem. At the present time, however, a vertical scarf similar to that shown in Figs. 84 and 97 usually is employed and the joint is reinforced by inserting a natural knee. Sometimes this knee goes in over the deadwood as in Fig. 84. In other cases, it constitutes the lowest piece of deadwood as in Fig. 97. In the lat-

FIG. 84—DETAILS OF STEM SHOWING LARGE NATURAL KNEE

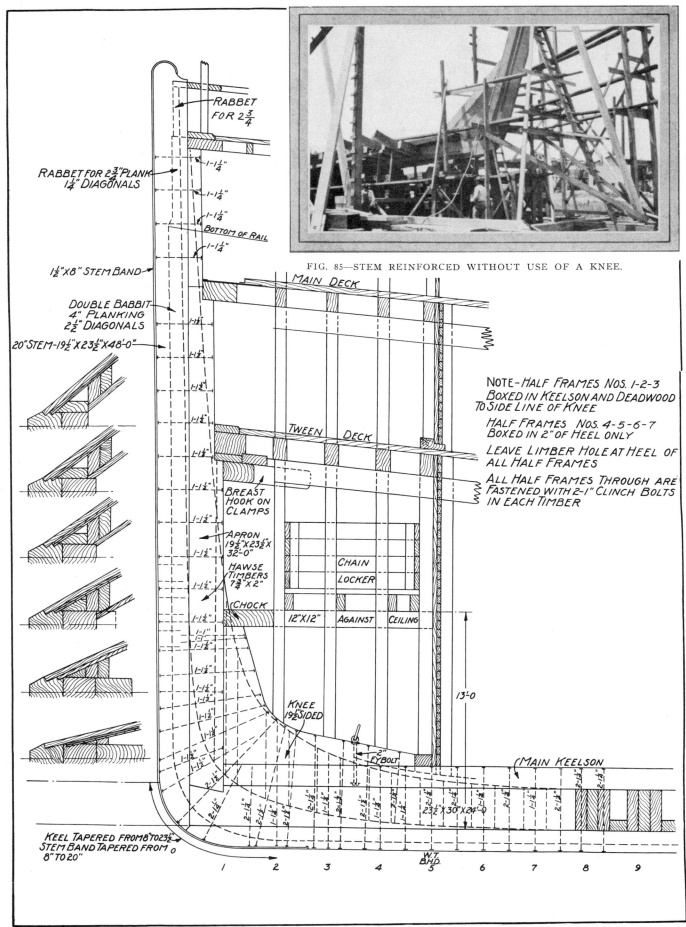

RABBET
FOR 2¾

RABBET FOR 2¾" PLANK
1¼ DIAGONALS

1-1¼"
1-1¼"
1-1¼"
BOTTOM OF RAIL
1-1¼"

1½"X8" STEM BAND

DOUBLE BABBIT
4" PLANKING
2½ DIAGONALS

20" STEM-19½"X23½"X48'-0"

1-1¼
1-1¼
1-1¼
1-1¼

TWEEN DECK

MAIN DECK

FIG. 85—STEM REINFORCED WITHOUT USE OF A KNEE.

NOTE-HALF FRAMES NOS. 1-2-3
BOXED IN KEELSON AND DEADWOOD
TO SIDE LINE OF KNEE

HALF FRAMES NOS. 4-5-6-7
BOXED IN 2" OF HEEL ONLY

LEAVE LIMBER HOLE AT HEEL OF
ALL HALF FRAMES

ALL HALF FRAMES THROUGH ARE
FASTENED WITH 2-1" CLINCH BOLTS
IN EACH TIMBER

1-1¼
1-1¼

BREAST
HOOK ON
CLAMPS

APRON
19½"X23½"X
32'-0"

HAWSE
TIMBERS
7¾"X 2"

CHOCK

CHAIN

LOCKER

12"X12"   AGAINST   CEILING

13'-0

KNEE
19½"SIDED

2"
EYBOLT

MAIN KEELSON

23½"X30"X24-0

KEEL TAPERED FROM 8 TO 23½
STEM BAND TAPERED FROM 0
8" TO 20"

1   2   3   4   W.T.   6   7   8   9
                        BHD.
                         5

FIG. 86—DETAILED DRAWING OF STEM OF A STEAMER THE GENERAL ARRANGEMENT OF WHICH IS SHOWN IN FIG. 84

FIG. 87—INTERIOR OF BOW CONSTRUCTION OF A 290-FOOT MOTOR SCHOONER. FIG. 88—DETAIL OF STEM CONSTRUC-
TION OF THE SCHOONER SHOWN IN FIG. 87 ILLUSTRATING METHOD OF FASTENING FORWARD ENDS OF
KEELSON TIMBERS TO STEM. FIG. 89—ARRANGEMENT OF STEM AND KNIGHTHEAD AT UPPER
END NEAR MAIN DECK. FIG. 90—STAGING SURROUNDING A CLIPPER-TYPE BOW
UNDER CONSTRUCTION

ter case, the knee usually is lock-scarfed, to the keel as shown.

The stem is trimmed to the proper curvature by means of molds sent from the mold-loft floor. These molds are made from the lines of the stem laid down on the floor when the sheer draft is prepared If the stem, or its counterpart, consists of more than one piece, a separate mold is made for each piece. In this case, it is a good idea to mark the waterlines on the mold, together with the two edges of rabbet and a vertical line by which to set the stem in its correct position. As many as a dozen separate molds were required for the clipper-type bows of some old English ships. At the present time, this has been reduced to two or three molds of the simplest character.

The stem usually has a tapered siding increasing uniformly from the fore end of the keel. In some cases, the taper extends to the top of the stem, while in others, when a particularly fine job is desired, three sidings are fixed, namely, at the head, midway down and at the keel.

After the stem piece is trimmed, in a manner to be described later, the several waterlines, fore edge of rabbet, bearding line and the vertical line for setting it in position, if it is of the clipper type, all are transferred to it from the molds. The rabbet is sometimes roughly cut before the stem is raised. It is advisable not to cut the rabbet to the exact depth but to leave enough wood to allow its being faired when the outside of the frame timbers are dubbed-off.

Raising the Stem

The stem, apron and knightheads are usually treenailed and bolted together before lifting them into place. For raising the stem a crane such as that employed for handling frames may be employed, or, if it is not available, a simple derrick or even nothing more than a gin pole may be used. After the stem is hoisted in place, if it is of the clipper type, its rake is proved by means of the vertical line marked upon it from the mold. It is set vertically by projecting the middle line of the keel sufficiently far forward to be below the most projecting part of the stem. Then if a plumb line, held against the middle line of stem at different heights, touches the line so produced, it is proof that the stem is vertical and free from any bulging or lateral curvature. After this fact is determined, the stem is securely shored into position. Where the stem is of the steamer type, its correct position in a transverse plane can readily be determined simply by dropping a plumb line from the upper end. The apron is really a portion of the stem, although it is distinguished from the stem proper by a separate name.

Its chief function is to back-up the stem, giving it additional strength and solidity.

Deadwood, as previously mentioned, is the name given to those pieces of timber which form the lean or acute portions of the bow and stern of the ship between the extremities and the cutting-down line, or line of the inside of timbers. This line generally bounds the upper side of the deadwood, the latter thus giving just the necessary amount of heeling for the cant timbers. But in very fine ships, the cutting-down line is sometimes on the keelsons, in order to save the great weight of timber at the extremities caused by making the deadwood deep enough of itself to receive the abutments of the cants.

Butts Should Give Good Shift

The pieces of which the deadwood is composed are arranged in such a manner that their butts give a good shift to each other and to those of the keel. When a floor crosses the deadwood, the lip of the deadwood scarf is so situated as to receive a through bolt, and in all cases the butts and scarfs are so placed as to be in the most favorable position to receive the fastenings. In both screw and sailing ships, the pieces of deadwood ought to be tenoned into the pieces of stern post that they abut against, and the former also should be doweled and bolted together, the dowels being spaced about a room and space apart.

In some cases, a mold for the deadwood is sent from the mold-loft floor. It is made of battens upon which the joints of the several pieces composing the deadwood are marked, together with the upper edge of rabbet or bearding line, the cutting-down line of the timbers and the positions of the heels of the cants and square frames. Half-section molds of the deadwood at several square stations also may be given. These can be tacked to the main mold so as to form a part of it, in such a position that the middle line of the half-section mold coincides with the line on the mold at which the section is given. The section molds generally give the form of the rabbet and the taper, if any, of the deadwood. The deadwood may be trimmed to the taper of the keel, stem or sternpost, although usually at the present time it has parallel siding. Its siding corresponds to that of the greatest siding of that portion of the keel upon which it rests. In any case, the marks on the mold, together with the sections, give the necessary data for trimming the several pieces.

The cant frames, Fig. 96, may be secured to the keel and deadwood with bolts which pass through and secure

the heels of the cants on the opposite side of the ship. These bolts usually are placed alternately high and low so as to avoid the weakness caused by a line of bolt holes. Sometimes the heels of all cants are scored into the deadwood, the line of the underside of the score being termed the stepping line. This has been done in the case of the cant shown in Fig. 96. Most modern shipbuilders, however, believe this labor is unnecessary, the cants being simply heeled against the keel and deadwood, without any such stepping. In such cases, however, the thin sliver edges of the foremost cant may be cut away and a piece of batten fitted in a score cut beneath. The batten can be fastened with short spikes and lightly caulked.

It would not be out of place to insert at this point a few remarks regarding methods of trimming ship timbers. At the present time, of course, the lumber is purchased from the mill cut as nearly to size as possible. Furthermore, the shipyard usually is equipped with planing, sawing and beveling machines which are adapted to perform a great number of operations rapidly and with mechanical accuracy. In many of the smaller yards, however, the mechanical equipment is limited, and skilled men who can do the work by hand are necessary. Also, around any shipyard there should be a few men who know how to trim a timber with an axe or adz and it will be found that the services of men of this character can always be made use of.

Operation Relatively Simple

No particular skill is required in trimming timbers in a machine, other than a knowledge of the principles on which the machine is operated and of the method of setting it for the work to be performed.

In practice, the trimming of timbers by hand includes the process of "lining the log" as well as the more mechanical operation of removing the superfluous wood with axe, adz, plane, etc. It is in the former sense only that we will consider the subject, as it is this portion of the work which involves thought and ingenuity.

Nearly all of the timbers from which a ship is built are so shaped that their cross sections are quadrilaterals, generally parallelograms. Also, the majority of the timbers have their opposite sides parallel, at least two of these generally being plane surfaces. As a result of these conditions, the process of trimming the several timbers of a ship is comparatively simple, consisting of the four following principal operations:

1.—Obtaining a fair surface, generally plane, upon one side of the timber.
2.—Molding the piece by applying the molds and then marking or setting off the curvature.

FIG. 91—DETAILS OF FOREFOOT SHOWING USE OF NATURAL KNEE AND ANGLE BLOCKS. FIG. 92—ANOTHER VIEW OF THE SAME STEM. FIG. 93—SAME STEM FROM THE OPPOSITE SIDE

3.—Trimming the two sides adjacent to the first by the aid of bevellings.
4.—Setting off the fourth side, if any, parallel to the first or at any required variable distance therefrom.

Since the piece of timber is supplied to the shipwright roughly in its required shape by the sawyer, the former usually can tell at a glance upon which side of the log the mold is to be applied.

A plane surface, technically termed "straight and out of winding" is obtained by striking a line along the side of the timber at the required position of the plane surface. A straight-edged batten is nailed against the end of the timber with its straight edge coinciding with the line just struck. The work-men then remove the wood above the line until the edge of a straight batten held everywhere along the trimmed surface of the timber is in the same plane as the edge of the batten nailed to the end of the timber. The battens when in the position just stated are said to be "out of winding." Incidentally, to accomplish this expeditiously requires more skill than usually is found in modern American shipyards.

A twisted surface, technically termed a winding surface, may be straight along one or both edges or may be curved; in either case, the curvature, if any, is first set off on the piece. The beveling spots also are marked and a straight-edged batten is nailed across an adjacent side at the middle beveling spot. A long-armed bevel, termed a punch bevel, is then set to the several bevelings of the twisted surface and the wood is removed on the side which is being trimmed as far as the edge lined off, until the long arm of the bevel, when held successively at the respective spots, is out of winding with the straight-edged batten, while at the same time the stock stays against the trimmed surface, the bevel being held square to the edge.

To trim a piece of timber having

FIG. 94—STEAMER TYPE BOW UNDER CONSTRUCTION, PARTLY PLANKED. FIG. 95—STEAMER TYPE BOW FINISHED WITH STAGING STILL IN PLACE. FIG. 96—FORWARD CANT FRAMES HEELING TO DEADWOOD

FIG. 97—DETAIL OF FOREFOOT OF CLIPPER TYPE STEM SHOWING
NATURAL KNEE LOCK-SCARFED TO KEEL

the points. This line will be one edge of the plane surface. Set off the siding of the timber from this line square to the edges of the batten and strike a line joining the siding spots; chamfer the edges away to these lines, to remove the surplus wood, with an axe or adz.

Siding the Timber

Now turn the timber over, having previously rased the positions of the battens over the ends. Repeat the operation of looking in points and lining the side, also of setting off the siding. Trim the two sides down from these lines to the chamfered edges. We thus have two plane sides to the timber, and if the sidings are uniform, the sides are also parallel. In its present state the timber is said to be sided.

This is one method of performing the operation. Others will occur to the experienced man. In modern wooden

straight siding and curved moldings, such as the stem or a beam, secure the piece upon blocks at a convenient height for trimming with the convex side nearest the ground. We may now proceed as follows:

Method of Procedure

Hold a straight-edged batten vertically against each end as near as possible to the side upon which the mold is to be made, so that lines joining the outer edges of the two battens, both above and below, may be everywhere within the log or timber. Adjust the battens so their edges are out of winding. Then, still looking these edges out of winding, determine points along the upper side of the timber which are in a line with the edges of the batten. Strike a line (this necessarily must be done in short lengths owing to the curvature of the side) along the upper side joining

FIG 99—DETAILS OF STEM AND FORWARD FRAME CONSTRUCTION OF A
MOTOR SCHOONER UNDER CONSTRUCTION ON THE GULF

FIG. 98—ARRANGEMENT OF FLOORS, KEELSON AND STEM OF A VESSEL
UNDER CONSTRUCTION AT A GULF SHIPYARD

shipyards, however, it is seldom necessary to resort to this rather elaborate process of siding a timber, machinery usually being available. However, as previously stated, it is well to know how the operation may be performed by hand.

For molding the curved shape of the timber, a mold is furnished from the mold loft. It is laid on the molding or joint side of the timber, being kept sufficiently *on* the surface to allow wood for obtaining the necessary beveling. Also due regard is had for the required length of the timber. In some cases, when concave curvature is given for convex timbers, as cant molds, for instance, the mold is held *off* the timber and the curvature is then copied by spiling. When the curvature is rased in and the positions of the beveling spots transferred, the mold is removed. the moldings of the timbers are set off, a

thin batten is set so it can pass fairly through the spots and the line so found is rased in.

Now set a bevel to each of the successive bevelings of the piece and apply the bevel to the molded edge, square to the curve and to the edge of the timber at the respective beveling spots. Hold the bevel so its tongue just touches the timber; measure with a pair of compasses the distance between the tongue and the molded edge and set this distance in upon the timber on the opposite side, measuring from the tongue. Bend the thin batten so as to pass through all of the points so obtained on the side opposite to the molded side, and rase in the line.

Trim the Curved Side

Now trim down the curved side of the timber straight from line to line, and the outer surface of the timber will be to its required state. The inside surface is trimmed parallel to the outer through the line obtained by setting off the molded scantlings. Frame timbers, beams, stem, apron, deadwood, sternposts of screw ships, etc., may be trimmed in this way if no machinery is available. A band-saw, however, as described in the previous chapter, is the proper tool to use for operations of this character. A knowledge of the method of marking, however, is just as necessary as if the work were to be done by hand.

A timber with straight siding and molding is trimmed by a simple and obvious modification of the methods just described. It is evident that the only difference consists in striking straight lines upon the plane surface instead of marking with a curved mold.

Fig. 83, in addition to illustrating the method of framing the bow and working up the stem of a clipper-type ship, also shows the staging which must be erected to give access to the sides of the ship during construction. This staging is similar to that used in house construction. The posts or stanchions usually are provided with holes bored about every foot so that the joists upon which the staging rests may be set at convenient heights. These holes also make it easy to take the staging down or to move it.

Figs. 87 and 88 show how the forward ends of the keelson are fastened to the stem, particularly in ships provided with heavy center girder-keelsons. It will be noted that the keelson timbers are securely bolted to the stem. These illustrations also show how the ceiling fays against the forward end of the center girder keelson.

A method of fastening the stem of a vessel to the keel without the use of a natural knee is shown in Fig. 85, illustrating the practice of a Gulf coast shipyard. It will be noted that in this case straight pieces of timber, suitably beveled at the ends, are inserted in place of the knee usually set in the corner formed by the keel and stem. This type of construction should be contrasted with that in which a knee is used, as illustrated in Fig. 97.

A well known method of working out the stem-to-keel connection in the case of a steamer type bow is illustrated in Figs. 91, 92 and 93. It will be noted that a natural knee is used to form the nose or forefoot of the ship and that the deadwood is reinforced by angle-blocking placed in the corner between the stem and the upper part of the deadwood. These illustrations also show clearly how the rabbet must be cut in the stem to receive the forward ends of the planking. More general views of a stem of this type in finished and semifinished states are shown respectively in Figs. 94 and 95.

Still another form of stem, using a very large natural knee in the angle, is illustrated in Fig. 84. A detailed drawing of this stem is presented in Fig. 86. This drawing shows the nature and disposition of the fastenings together with the arrangement of the stem, keel, apron, deadwood, knee, etc. The drawing should be studied carefully. Cross sections of the stem, apron, knighthead and forward frames at various waterline elevations are shown on the drawing. It will be noted that two rabbets are provided, this ship being triple planked with an inner skin of double diagonals and an outer skin of ordinary horizontal planking. The large wooden knee set in the angle of the stem is sided 19½ inches. The horizontal leg of this knee is 11 feet in length, the vertical leg being 8 feet. Half frames Nos. 1, 2 and 3, Fig. 86, are boxed in the keelson and deadwood to the sidelines of the knee. Half frames Nos. 4, 5, 6 and 7 are boxed in 2 inches at the heel only. Limber holes are left at the heels of all the half frames. The half frames are screw fastened with two 1-inch clinch bolts in each timber.

CHAPTER VII

Framing the After End of the Ship

STERN framing involves many problems, not only on account of the large number of pieces necessary to build up the stern of a wooden vessel, but also because of the number of different types of sterns in use. In fact, it is the stern which gives character to the entire vessel and here we find the most distinctive lines. This has been true of naval architecture in every age. The old Spanish galleons were not specially different in many of their elements from modern wooden ships. They are famous, however, for their exceedingly bizarre, high awkward sterns. The same remarks apply to the Chinese luggers that infest the Yellow sea.

In fact, just as different periods have produced their particular forms of land architecture, so there has been a succession of styles in naval architecture, each of which has grown out of that preceding it. And, as in the case of land architecture, the latest style is preferred for a period as being more beautiful and useful; it gives way, however, in time to other styles which are considered superior to it. In no part of a wooden ship have these differences in style been more marked than at the stern and the problems of construction have been

FIG. 100—DETAIL OF STERN FRAME OF SHIP BEING BUILT FOR UNITED STATES GOVERNMENT

similarly influenced. Today, therefore, we have several different types of sterns in service. Most American wooden ship builders prefer the square or transom stern. This stern may be made either with or without quarter blocks. A good example of the former type is shown in Fig. 124. A transom stern of the latter type, framed without the use of quarter blocks, is shown in Fig. 101.

For steamers and full-powered mo-

tor ships many builders prefer the fantail or elliptical stern. Examples of this stern are shown in Figs. 105, 119 and 125. In fact, this type of stern is so popular with steam ship builders that it might be called the steamer type of stern, just as the straight stem forms the steamer-type bow. We also have conical sterns, which when properly designed are unusually graceful, as well as the parabolic or cruiser-type stern. Practically no wooden ships have been built with sterns of the latter two types.

In all sterns, the combination of frames is uniform as far aft as the sternpost. Up to this point, the framing is nothing more than a cant arrangement. In both the elliptical and transom sterns, the last of these cants is termed a fashion timber. It is so disposed that the various elements of the stern framing proper can heel against it. The fashion timber of a transom stern is shown very clearly in Fig. 107. This illustration, together with Figs. 108, 109 and 110, shows the details of one method of framing a transom stern. The transom stern is sufficiently important to justify a detailed description of one method of timbering

FIG. 101—FINISHING TRANSOM STERN ON A 5-MASTED MOTOR SCHOONER. FIG. 102—DETAIL OF RUDDER AND RUDDERPOST ASSEMBLY

FIG. 103—DETAIL OF UPPER PART OF STERN FRAMING SHOWN IN FIG. 102. FIG. 104—GENERAL VIEW OF STERN FRAMES AND RUDDER ASSEMBLY

it. As previously stated, this type of stern is sometimes called the square stern. Abaft the fashion timber it may be composed of two sets of timbers as follows:

1.—Horizontal timbers, extending from fashion timber to fashion timber and scoring into the stern post. These are termed transoms.
2.—Vertical timbers, extending from the upper transom to the rail. These pieces, which are termed stern timbers, are shown in Fig. 108.

The farthest of these stern timbers from the middle line, the one which partakes of the rake of the stern and

also of that of the topside, is termed the side-counter timber. It is shown in Fig. 107. It heels against the upper transom and fays against the fashion timbers.

In some ships, the transom timbers situated at certain positions are distinguished by particular names. The one which forms the base of the stern, that is the transom upon which the stern timbers step and to which they may be tenoned, is termed the wing transom. Boxen wood is left on the edge of this timber in order

to house the planks of the bottom and to receive the fastenings of their hooding ends. The line at which the planks end is called the margin; and a rail called the tuck rail is fitted over the boxen left above the margin, thus giving a finished appearance at the ends of the planking. This method of finishing the planking, slightly modified, is shown in Fig. 101.

In some large ships, the principal transom is called the deck transom. It is situated at the height of the deck and its upper surface conforms

FIG. 105—ERECTING FORE AND AFT POST TIMBERS FOR A STERN OF UNUSUALLY STRONG CONSTRUCTION

FIG. 106—DETAIL OF TRANSOM STERN FRAMING OF A SHIP UNDER CONSTRUCTION IN A SOUTHERN YARD. FIG. 107—TRANSOM TYPE STERN IN EARLY STAGES OF CONSTRUCTION. FIG. 108—THE NEXT STEP IN THE CONSTRUCTION OF A TRANSOM STERN. FIG. 109—INTERIOR OF A TRANSOM STERN BEFORE TRANSOM TIMBERS ARE IN PLACE. FIG. 110—A CLOSER VIEW OF THE INTERIOR OF THE SAME STERN. FIG. 111—FITTING TRANSOM TIMBERS TO FASHION TIMBER

FIG. 112—STERN FRAME ASSEMBLY BEING HOISTED INTO PLACE

All except the deck and wing transoms have their upper and lower surfaces in a plane which is either horizontal, or square to the after side of the stern post. The deck and wing transoms, however, have their sides trimmed to a surface which partakes of the round of the beam and the sheer of the topsides and deck respectively.

A Trim, Neat Stern

Although certain English writers on naval architecture seem to take pleasure in sneering at the transom stern on the ground that it is ungainly and unworkmanlike in appearance, it can, nevertheless, be made very trim and neat, as Fig. 101 clearly indicates. Also it is relatively simple to construct, cheap, and easily repaired in case of damage. In addition, it offers good resistance to a heavy following

to the round up of the beams, being made sufficiently wide to receive the fastenings of the deck planks which stop at a rabbet or score in it. Between the wing and deck transoms certain others are fitted, the number being regulated by the distance between the two main beams. These usually are called filling transoms.

Below the deck transom a series of other transoms may be fitted, sufficient in number to extend from the deck transom to a short distance above the heel of the fashion timber, the space between the lowest and the bearding line being filled in by short canted timbers which are tenoned to the under-side of the lowest transom.

In ships of this character, the transoms below the deck transom are distinguished by number, according to the order of their position below it.

FIG. 114—INSIDE OF FRAMING OF THE STERN SHOWN IN FIG. 113

FIG. 113—DETAIL OF FRAMING OF TRANSOM TYPE STERN

sea. When not hampered by too many restrictions, a good naval architect likes to give earnest consideration to the beauty of his vessel. To accomplish this, special attention is paid to the form of the stern and as already indicated, some architects prefer the elliptical type to the transom type just discussed. Its framing is similar to the transom stern up to the fashion timber. Beyond this point, the framing differs radically.

The upper aftermost portion of the continuation of the contour of the ship's bottom is termed the buttock. It is usually so flat and nearly horizontal that the only planes which give a definite intersection with it on the drafting board are the vertical longitudinal or buttock planes. Therefore, the buttock lines are of considerable service and are largely employed in

FIG. 115—DETAIL OF STERN FRAMING FROM THE INSIDE OF A SHIP. FIG. 116—ANOTHER VIEW OF THE FRAMING OF THE SAME SHIP   FIG. 117—LOWER PART OF STERN FRAMING OF THE SAME SHIP SHOWING STERN-POST, DEADWOOD, ETC.   FIG. 118—SAME STERN PLANKED UP AND NEARLY FINISHED

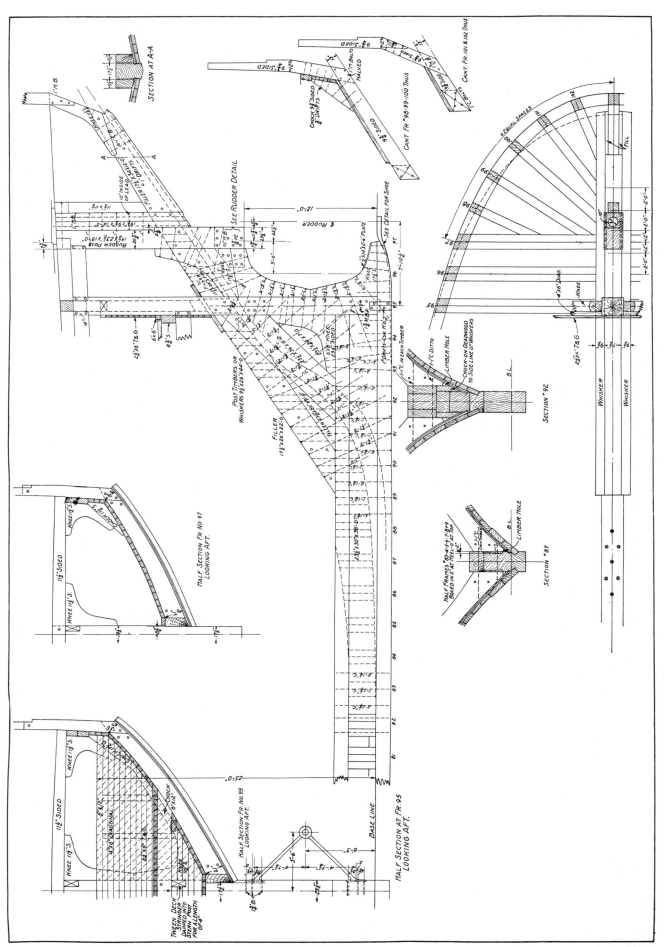

FIG. 110—DETAILS OF THE ELLIPTICAL OR FANTAIL STERN SHOWN IN FIGS 105 AND 125

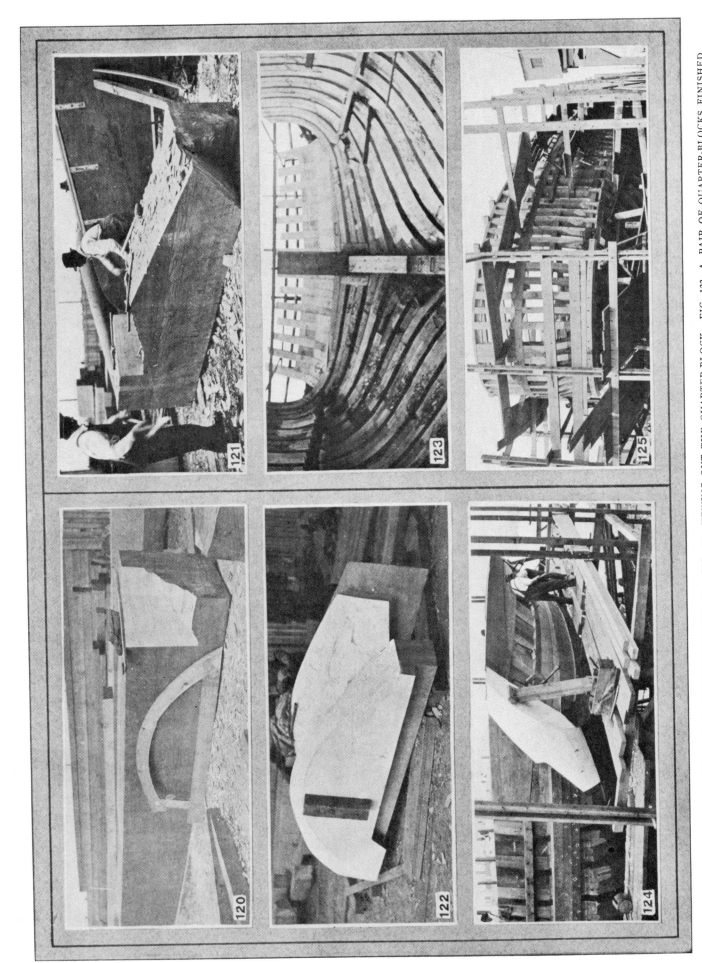

FIG. 120—TIMBER FROM WHICH QUARTER-BLOCK IS HEWED. FIG. 121—HEWING OUT THE QUARTER-BLOCK. FIG. 122—A PAIR OF QUARTER-BLOCKS FINISHED. FIG. 123—QUARTER-BLOCK IN PLACE. FIG. 124—QUARTER-BLOCK LEFT FOR RECEPTION OF QUARTER BLOCKS. FIG. 125—GENERAL VIEW OF ELLIPTICAL OR FANTAIL STERN

fairing this portion of the ship, either in the drawing room or on the mold-loft floor, as described in considerable detail in the fifth chapter of this book pages 41 and 43. The buttock lines afford a very accurate conception of the nature of the surface, when studied by an experienced man.

The elliptical stern, when viewed in the sheer plan, rakes aft, the boundary line being straight and making an obtuse angle with the line forming the boundary of the buttock. This angle, which is continued around the stern until the curvature of the buttock breaks continuously into the inward inclination of the ship's side, is

sides of the stern timbers are then inclined so as to be straight lines on this cone. These lines, if produced, will pass through the apex.

The character of the cone is governed by the rake of the stern right aft and the tumble-home of the side as well as by the curvature of the knuckle line. The after extremities of the topside or rail form curves approximating those of an ellipse. Hence the name elliptical stern is given to this style of construction.

The surface of the stern above the knuckle, being approximately an elliptical cone, and the surface of the stern below the knuckle a continua-

short cants which, like the quarter-timbers, are heeled upon the fashion timber. Quarter-timbers and those abaft them are known by the generic name of stern timbers. In disposing these stern timbers it is necessary that they should be canted in such positions as will avoid excessive beveling. At the same time it is necessary for the timbers to heel on the fashion timber or on a short cant which itself heels upon another stern timber. Sometimes it is necessary to give the stern timbers a double cant.

The chief feature of the parabolic stern is the absence of a knuckle. This stern, therefore, becomes a con-

FIG. 126—ANOTHER VIEW OF THE STERN SHOWN IN FIG. 125. FIG. 127—NATURAL KNEE USED TO CONNECT STERN-POST TO OTHER STERN ELEMENTS. FIG. 128—SHAFT LOG IN TWIN-SCREW MOTOR SHIP

termed the knuckle. This knuckle is shown clearly in Fig. 129. In the sheer draft, showing the lines of the ship, it is called the knuckle line.

Now on account of the inward inclination or tumble-home of the ship's side and the rake of the stern right aft, the surface of the ship's side between these limits must necessarily be twisted. Now it has been found that if square openings are cut in such a stern they are very unsightly. Round portholes, therefore, are much to be preferred.

In order to give this type of stern a still more pleasing appearance, the following procedure may be adopted. Produce upward indefinitely the line of rake right aft. Now draw a line from the end of the knuckle line in the direction of the tumble-home of the side. The point of intersection of these lines may be chosen as the apex of a cone containing the knuckle line and enveloping the stern. The

tion of the contour of the ship's bottom, it remains to be decided just what kind of a line the knuckle shall be. It is evident that although the former surface may be invariable, it is possible to modify the surface of the bottom, consistent with fairness, so that the position of the knuckle may be varied slightly to suit appearances. It is customary to place the knuckle line in the surface containing the upper sides of the beams of a deck, both for the sake of beauty and to suit the internal arrangements of the ship. Therefore, the knuckle line conforms to the round of the beam and the sheer of the deck.

In disposing the timbers in an elliptical type stern, the quarter timbers are so placed that their edges are straight lines on the cone surface just where the latter blends into the surface of the topside. Spaces between these and the aftermost fashion timber are filled up by a number of

tinuation of the buttock, the post timbers forming the backbone, as it were, of the ship abaft the body post. These timbers are close jointed from the gunwale to the body post. Boxen wood is left on the post timbers to house the aftermost ends of the side and bottom planks in this form of construction. Instead of the complicated arrangement of timbers required by the systems previously described, the framing of this type of stern consists of ordinary cants. Those before the screw aperture heel against the deadwood and those abaft it heel against the sides of the post timbers. It is not necessary to go into detail regarding methods of laying off these timbers. The post timbers are laid off in the sheer plan on the mold loft and the remaining timbers, as previously stated, are ordinary cants.

In most modern wooden ships the sternpost simply heels square against the keel and after ends of deadwood.

FIG. 129—DETAIL OF FANTAIL STERN CONSTRUCTION AT KNUCKLE LINE

Frequently a heavy wooden knee is inserted in the angle between the post and upper side of the deadwood. This construction is clearly shown in Fig. 119.

The sternpost and other sections of the stern frame may be raised into position with a traveling crane such as that previously described for handling frames and bow timbers, or, if necessary, simple derricks, or gin poles may be used. After the sternpost is in place it may be used to support the tackle employed to handle some of the other timbers.

Most ship builders raise the rudderpost by itself, hanging the rudder later. In some cases, however, the rudder is assembled to the rudderpost on the ground and the whole combination raised at one time. This method of raising the rudder and rudderpost, together with the fashion timber in a single assembly is shown clearly in Figs. 102 and 104. It is said by the builder that this method of handling the problem saves $50 in labor cost. Fig. 104 shows clearly how the assembly looks before the after cant frames and stern timbers are in place. A more detailed view is shown in Fig. 102.

Handling Small Stern Timbers

For handling the smaller stern timbers, simple block and tackle arrangements such as those illustrated in Figs. 110, 111 and 112, usually are employed. These illustrations show various stages of the stern framing of a transom-stern, 5-masted auxiliary schooner built at the plant of the Grays Harbor Shipbuilding Co., Aberdeen, Wash.

Fig. 112 is particularly instructive. It will be noted that the irregular pieces of stern timber are hewed out, beveled and assembled as far as possible on the ground. The various sections are fastened together by iron drift bolts. The assembly is then hoisted into place with a block and tackle connected to an eye bolt which is temporarily screwed into the piece. After the assembly is bolted in its proper place in the ship, the eye bolt is removed.

The various stages in framing the transom stern shown in Fig. 101 are clearly illustrated by Figs. 107, 108, 109, 110, 111, 112 and 118. Fig. 107 shows the framing before the transom timbers are in place. In Fig. 108 part of these timbers have been set in their proper positions, Figs. 109 and 110 show inside views of the same stern. In the latter, the arrangement of the sternpost and aftermost frames is clearly indicated. Fig. 109 shows how the ceiling fits up against the keelson and sternpost in the after part of the ship. The method of assembling some of the transom sections will be understood by studying Figs. 111 and 112.

The framing of a transom stern in a schooner building in a Georgia shipyard is shown in Fig. 106. In this case, natural bent crooks are used which adds considerably to the strength of the structure. The deckhouse shown in Fig. 101 protects the steering gear. The character of the scaffolding necessary around the stern when the ship is under construction is shown clearly in Figs. 107, 108 and 118. The latter illustration shows a transom stern planked up and nearly completed. As shown in Fig. 113, the side counter timbers are double. The triangular space between them and the aftermost frame is filled in with short cants which heel against the side counter timbers. These pieces, or cants usually are sided about 8 inches and molded about 10 inches. Until the planking is bolted in place, they are lightly spiked to a ribband, as shown in Fig. 113. The interior of this part of the same stern is shown in Fig. 114, which also illustrates the after main frames and the arrangement of the deck beams in the way of the stern. Further details of this type of stern framing, in an earlier stage of the construction process, are shown in Figs. 115 and 116. These illustrations show quite clearly how the after stern frames are formed and how they heel against the sternpost and after portion of the deadwood. The arrangement of the ceiling near the stern post also is suggested.

Lower Part of Stern

The lower part of this same stern is shown in Fig. 117. This illustration clearly indicates the arrangement

FIG. 130—ARRANGEMENT OF TIMBERS INSIDE THE SAME STERN AT THE POINT SHOWN IN FIG. 129

of the sternpost, deadwood and the heels of the after frames. The three bronze sockets for the rudder pintles also are shown. In addition, the shaft log for one of the twin screws may be seen at the extreme left of the illustration.

In another form of transom stern, illustrated in Figs. 120 to 124, inclusive, a quarter-block is employed to fill out the corners of the transom, instead of using short cants heeling against the side counter timber, as shown in Fig. 113. Some builders think the quarter-block construction is neater. Also it saves considerable detail work in fitting up the framing and is a help to the designer if he is a little shy on geometry. But as indicated by Fig. 120, the quarter-block is rather wasteful of timber. This illustration shows the baulk from which the block is hewed. A piece 36 inches square and about 10 feet long is required to make each block. One of the curved molds from which the block is hewed is shown in the foreground of Fig. 120.

Fig. 121 shows the quarter-block being hewed out. Two men are employed and it is essential that they have considerable skill in order to turn out a neatly finished block. Two completed blocks, ready to go into the ship, are shown in Fig. 122. The strip shown nailed on the side of the block is placed there simply for convenience in handling. A detail of the arrangement of the frames in the way of the stern, showing the holes left for the reception of the quarter-blocks is shown in Fig. 123. Fig. 124 shows the block in place, and indicates how the after-ends of the planking close against the rabbet formed by the block. This illustration also shows clearly how the transom is framed, using clamps to hold the planks in place before they are spiked down.

A Fantail Stern

The details of a neatly formed elliptical or fantail stern are shown in Figs. 125 to 127. Figs. 129 and 130 show close-up details of the same stern. This stern is framed with timbers sided 7¾ inches. The details of the knuckle joints are clearly shown in Fig. 129, the interior of the same joints being illustrated by Fig. 130. Bolted construction is employed.

The fastenings and other details of this stern are shown completely in Fig. 119. As this illustration indicates, liberal use is made of natural knees, there being three fayed against the sternpost and one against the rudderpost. As Fig. 119 also indicates, the various parts are very thoroughly drift-bolted together. The sternpost is 23½ x 19½ inches in section and 30 feet in length. The rudderpost is 19½ x 23½ inches in section, the same as the sternpost, and 18 feet in length. The main piece of deadwood is 23½ x 30 inches, 38 feet in length. The knee which fills the angle between the sternpost and deadwood is 6 x 6 feet, sided 23½ inches.

In general, it will be noted that this stern consists of cant frames stepping on two fore and aft post timbers or whiskers. These timbers, as indicated by Fig. 119, are 9½ x 26 inches in cross section and 44 feet in length. They are notched into the sternpost and rudderpost and are continuous from the deadwood to the knuckle line. The space between the post timbers is taken up by filling blocks sided 17½ inches. The general arrangement of the fore and aft post timbers or whiskers is shown clearly in Fig. 105, which illustrates this stern in an early stage of construction. The post timbers are equivalent to a continuation of the deadwood and the aftermost cant frames heel against them.

Fig. 128 shows how the shaft log comes through the stern frame on a twin-screw motor ship. In this case, the log consists of two timbers bolted and doweled together. The outer end of the shaft, just ahead of the propeller, is further steadied by a steel truss, the details of which are shown in Fig. 119.

CHAPTER VIII

Planking, Keelson and Ceiling Construction

AFTER the frames, stem, stern-post, etc., are all set in place, the ship is ready to be planked on the outside and ceiled on the inside. The keelson construction on the inside also can be finished. Next to the frames, the exterior planking probably is the most important part of the ship's structure. In the old days, the planking of large ships was divided into a number of distinct assemblies each with a special designation. Old-line wooden ship builders accordingly were familiar with such terms as sheer strakes, channel and middle wales, black strakes, main wales, diminishing planks, plank of bottom, and garboard strakes. These names are given in the order of the respective assemblages, beginning at the topside. In the old warships, the sheer strakes were situated between the planksheer or covering plank and the ports of the main deck. Below the latter, as far as the ports of the middle deck, the external planks were termed channel wales, as they received the fastenings of the chain plate and preventer bolts of the channels. The

FIG. 131—TIMBER CHUTE FOR HAUL-ING CEILING STRAKES AND KEEL-SONS INSIDE THE SHIP

middle wales were situated between the ports of the middle and lower decks, while the planks immediately below the lower deck ports were termed black strakes, owing to the fact that their upper edges formed the boundary line of the portion of the ship below the fighting decks, which was painted black. From the main wales, the planks gradually diminished in thickness to that of the plank-of-bottom strakes. The strakes in which taper was worked were known as diminishing plank. The plank-of-bottom extended from the diminishing plank to the garboard strake, the lower edge of the latter rabbeting to the keel. The planks between the ports were termed short stuff, being specially designated according to their situation as short stuff 'tween decks, etc.

Modern ship builders have forgotten all about these terms and at the present time about all we hear of are garboards, bottom plank and topside planking. In some cases bilge plank-ing is mentioned. The planking usual-ly is arranged in a series of strakes of diminishing thickness, the garboard strakes adjoining keel being thickest. Before starting in to plank a ship, a disposition of the edges and butts

FIG. 132—INTERIOR OF A WOODEN SHIP UNDER CONSTRUCTION SHOWING TIMBER CHUTE AND SCAFFOLDING—BILGE
CEILING IN PLACE

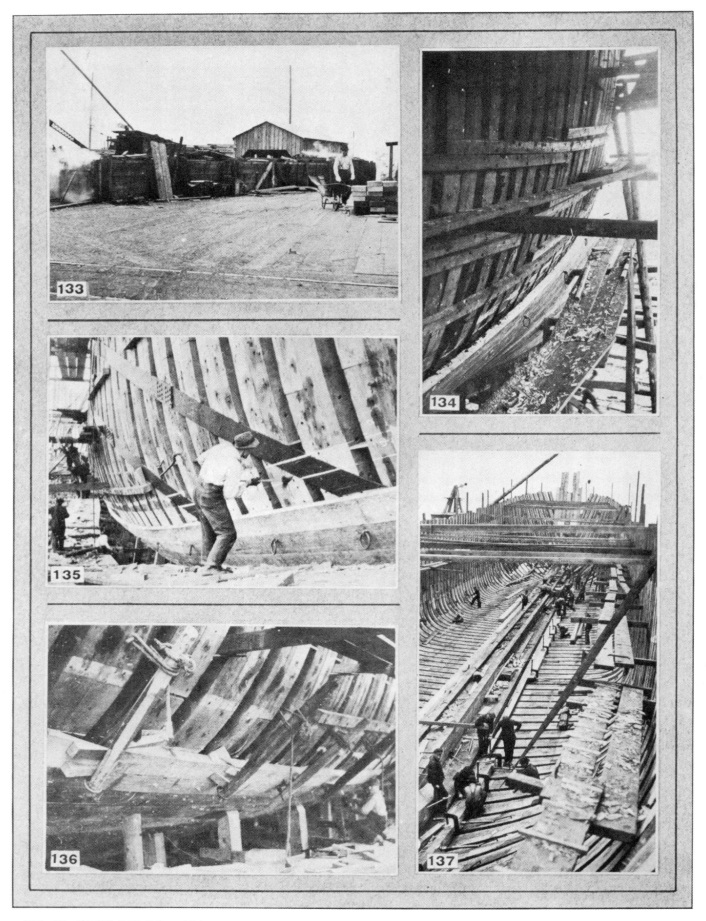

FIG. 133—STEAM BOX FOR SOFTENING PLANKS. FIG. 134— SIDE OF SHIP WITH PLANK IN PLACE. FIG. 135—DUBBING-OFF AND RASING LINES ON SHIP'S SIDE FOR PLANKING. FIG. 136—CLAMPING PLANK IN PLACE PRIOR TO SPIKING. FIG. 137—CLAMPING CEILING STRAKES IN PLACE PRIOR TO BOLTING

FIG. 138—LOWER ENDS OF STERN FRAME AND DEADWOOD RASED FOR PLANKING

case may be, is termed a stealer.

The lengths of the planks should be as great as can be obtained. In England three strakes are placed between consecutive butts on the same frame. This practice is not followed in the United States, where one strake in many cases is considered sufficient. Two, however, is better practice. The butts also should be disposed so as to avoid the succession suggested by the name ladder step.

Lloyd's rules do not permit the butts to be nearer than 5 feet from each other, unless there is a strake wrought between them and then a distance of 4 feet is allowed. No butts are permitted on the same timber unless there are three strakes between them. In ships with extreme proportions the figures six and five are substituted for five and four, respectively.

In most yards in the United States,

should be prepared and set off on an expansion drawing. If care is taken in arranging disposition of the planks, considerable work can be avoided. Planks between the main deck and the keel should be filled up in such a way as to give the least possible twist or curvature, thus simplifying the conversion of the material and work of securing the planks in place.

In a full-bodied ship it will be found impossible to continue the same number of planks right fore and aft, owing to the difference between the girth amidships and at the extremities. In every case, in fact, there is a considerable reduction in the breadths of the planks before they terminate at the stem or stern. When it is necessary to reduce the number of planks for the reason just mentioned, the last plank of the strake which does not extend right fore and aft, as the

FIG. 140—BOLTING DOWN KEELSON TIMBERS WITH PNEUMATIC HAMMERS

FIG. 139—CEILING A SHIP IN A GULF COAST YARD

the vessel is planked from the keel upward. Sometimes, however, the garboard strakes and the wales at the top are first put on and the planking then proceeds from both top and bottom toward the bilges.

Before working the planks, the lines of their edges are rased in on the frames by means of battens bent in the position indicated by the expansion drawings. Fig. 138 shows how these lines are rased on the keel and lower ends of the frames and after deadwood. Fig. 135 shows how the lines are rased on the frames amidship. The latter illustration also shows how the frames are dubbed-off to a fair surface before the planks are spiked in place. The dubbing-off operation is performed by skilled workmen using an adz. It is a rather expensive process and recently some interesting experiments have been

made with a machine designed to perform this operation. This machine, a portable electrically driven planer, with circular knives, works something on the principle of a lawn-mower. It is said to save a tremendous amount of time in dubbing-off the outer surface of the ship.

A True Sheer Necessary

Care must be taken in rasing in the lines shown in Figs. 135 and 138 that the front or sight-edge of the plank is the line drawn, as at the bow and buttock where there is a considerable twist in the surface, a very unsightly edge and not the true sheer would

ness of the plank, the diminution being, however, only about ⅛ inch in 12 inches.

For the extremities of the ship and on the bilges it is necessary to soften the planks by steaming them in a steam box provided for that purpose. A box of this character is shown in Fig. 133. It is 90 feet in length and about 6 feet square, built of large timbers edge-bolted together and caulked. The necessary steam is supplied at low pressure by an ordinary donkey boiler fired with refuse wood from the shipyard. In many yards the hot plank is often transferred from the steam box to the ship by hand.

ner shown in Fig. 136. Before the plank is clamped in place, the bottoms of the holes which are to receive the spikes are reamed out with a hand auger so the spikes may be set easily. The plank is first tacked or stuck in position with 10-inch galvanized boat spikes which are driven by hand. Two spikes are driven at the ends and one in between on every frame. After these spikes are driven, the shores and wedges may be removed. The ring bolts also can be taken out, leaving the planking as it appears in Fig. 134. It is now ready to receive the final fastenings which usually consist of locust treenails and iron drift-bolts.

FIG. 141—PORT SIDE OF A COMPLETELY CEILED WOODEN MOTOR SHIP

be obtained if this precaution were not observed.

The edges of the planks are trimmed square to the surface of the timbers, this being expressed in technical language by saying that the "closest edges stand between two squares". A little deduction is made from this angle to allow for the caulking seams. Usually it amounts to 1/16 inch to every inch of plank thickness, when the plank does not exceed 6 inches in thickness, which is rare in modern shipbuilding. One method of determining the seam adopted by workmen is to set the two arms of a 2-foot rule ⅝ inch apart at their extremities. This gives rather less than 1/16 inch of seam for every inch in the thick-

In most Pacific coast shipyards a gang of 12 men is employed for planking the ship. A gang of this sort, with some additional labor, should be able to plank up one strake a day clear around a 275-foot ship from the keel to the bilges. From this point up to the rail the planking should proceed at the rate of two strakes per day, allowing 35 days altogether to plank the ship.

Putting on the Plank

The necessary holes for the fastenings are bored in the plank before it is brought out to the ship. After being lifted into place, the plank is tightened into position by means of chains, shores and wedges in the man-

The treenails, which are about 26 inches long and 1¼ inches in diameter, are driven into holes bored a scant 1¼ inches. After they are driven home, they are wedged on the ends and in some cases caulked. Special care is required in driving treenails in order to avoid crippling them, as in this case it is impossible to drive them any further and they must either be driven or bored out and their places supplied by others which generally are less efficient than if driven through in the first place. Treenails should be of well-seasoned sound locust or oak cut with the grain.

There is a considerable difference of opinion regarding the comparative value of treenail and drift-bolt fasten-

FIG. 142—BEVELING KEELSON TIMBERS BY HAND. FIG. 143—MAKING A SCARF IN A KEELSON TIMBER. FIG. 144—THE FIRST STEP IN BUILDING UP A CENTER GIRDER-KEELSON. FIG. 145—CLAMPS USED FOR TEMPORARILY SECURING KEELSON PIECES. FIG. 146—BORING DRIFTBOLT HOLES IN CENTER GIRDER-KEELSON. FIG. 147—CENTER GIRDER-KEELSON NEARLY COMPLETED

FIG. 148—CEILING STRAKES ON TABLE OF AUTOMATIC BEVELING MACHINE—NOTE BATTEN ALONG TOP WHICH INDICATES THE AMOUNT OF BEVEL

FIG. 149—IN SOME YARDS THE CEILING IS LAID IN PARALLEL STRAKES BETWEEN THE KEELSONS AND THE BILGE.
FIG. 150—DUBBING-OFF THE INSIDE PREPARATORY TO CEILING

FIG. 151—KEELSON CONSTRUCTION OF A SMALL MOTOR SCHOONER

ings. Some modern authorities incline to the opinion that treenails are practically worthless. Nevertheless, they are very largely employed. An English authority expresses himself on this subject as follows: "The superior lightness and cheapness of the

treenails, being restricted only as regards the butts, each of which must be fastened by two bolts, one of which should extend through and be clenched. A year is deducted from the ship's period when the latter condition is not fulfilled. It should be

chalk marks on the planks where the steel straps and other iron work are situated so that the fastenings may be set off clear of them. When the positions of these fastenings are discovered, then the remainder of the fastenings of the planks can be set off.

FIG. 152—CLAMPING AND BOLTING UPPER CEILING STRAKES IN PLACE

treenail are obvious, but its superiority in point of strength is questionable. There is no doubt but that a well-made and tightly-driven treenail, of sound, seasoned oak, possesses considerable holding power when caulked at both ends; and it is not subject to the deterioration due to the action of the acids in the timber, which is so common with iron fastenings. But when the inferior resistance to sheering, the weakening of the frame timbers caused by boring such large holes as treenails require, also their tendency to draw in the process of caulking the plank are all taken into account, there is undoubtedly a large margin of efficiency in favor of the through metal fastenings. When the latter are of copper or mixed metal, the inferiority of the treenail is established in all respects, except as regards cost and weight. The clauses in Lloyd's rules referring to this subject are probably founded on these conclusions."

Using More Metal

It might be stated that American ship builders rarely, if ever, employ copper or mixed metal fastenings, owing to their excessive cost. Gradually, however, ship builders are using more and more steel drift bolts and spikes in place of treenails on account of their superior strength and holding power.

According to Lloyd's rules, the builder is at liberty to decide what proportion of his fastenings shall be

observed that one of these bolts is placed through the butt timber and the other in the timber adjacent to it. The rules require further that two-thirds of the bolts and treenails shall be driven through, the former being

As previously stated, the edges of the planks are rased on the timbers in order to be sure that they will conform to the sheer of the ship, thus assisting in giving her a graceful appearance. In this connection, it may be noted that if a wide batten, termed a spiling batten, be bent around the ship's side, especially at the bow and stern, it will be found that it will not bend to the curves of some of the lines. The latter are sometimes either convex or concave with reference to the upper edge of the spiling batten. In the former case the edge is said to have sny and in the latter, hang.

Determining Sny and Hang

Now the first operation in taking account of a strake of planks is to determine the amount of sny or hang in the edge of the adjacent plank against which the plank to be trimmed must be fitted. This may be accomplished in the following manner:

Bend a spiling batten fairly upon the timbers just above and as near as possible to the upper edge of the last plank in place so that the edges of the batten are unrestrained. Now

FIG. 153—CEILING A SHIP IN THE WAY OF THE STERN, SHOWING THE USE OF CLAMPS

clenched on rings on the inside, and the latter caulked and wedged on the outer plank and ceiling.

Before setting off the fastenings, it is necessary to bore off from the inside of the ship all of the through fastenings for shelves, waterways, beams, knees, etc., and to indicate by

choose a certain number of beveling and spiling spots, say, one at every frame stage, and mark them both upon the batten and the timbers. Then measure the distance from the lower edge of the spiling staff to the upper edge of the plank at each of the spiling spots. Transfer the spiling

spots to the plank. Now bend a batten to pass through the points thus obtained and so draw the line of the inner lower edge of the plank. The upper edge is obtained by measuring on the plank the distance to the line of the upper edge rased upon the timbers at the several spiling spots. These breadths should be set off at the respective spiling spots on the planks and a curve passed through the points. The planks may now be trimmed to a square beveling minus half the allowance for the caulking seam.

In case the strake is a shutter-in, or the last strake to go in place, the spilings for the width may be taken by means of small pieces of stick cut so as to fit tightly between the two strakes, close against the timbers. The breadths of the plank at the several spiling spots are set off by means of these sticks. The bevelings of the upper edge are obtained in the same way as those of the lower. In case the plank is the last one to complete a strake and is therefore a shutter in lengthwise, an addition to the foregoing precaution is necessary. In this case it is advisable to leave one butt uncut until after the plank is nearly bent and shored in place, the other butt being driven home closely against its neighbor. Now bend a light batten and measure the girth of the ship against the timbers, from the last point where the plank touches them to the butt of the adjacent plank of the strake against which the butt about to be cut must fit, and mark the latter point on the batten. Then, still keeping the first end of the batten fixed, let it spring along the inner surface of the plank and mark the point upon the latter. Cut the butt at this point.

Keelson Timbers

Keelsons are made from long timbers similar to keel pieces. In some yards they are bevelled by hand, as shown by Fig. 142, a skilled workman being necessary for this operation. The scarfs at the end, in cases where the keelsons consist of two or more pieces, are made in the manner shown in Fig. 143.

In some of the more modern yards, the keelson timbers and ceiling are beveled on a machine, as shown in Fig. 148. This shows two 7 x 14-inch x 80-foot timbers resting on the traveling table of the beveling machine. A batten is nailed the full length of

the timbers in order to indicate the correct bevel. The side-head of the machine is set so that the bevel is cut fair with the batten. The timber is held against the side-head by means of a special roll shown in the background in Fig. 148.

This machine was designed and built by the Stetson Machine Works, Seattle. The machine consists essentially of a beveling side-head, shown at the left in the background in Fig. 148, a beveling top-head and a roller table for handling the material. The machine may be driven by individual motor or it may be connected to an existing system of line shafting. The side-head, which is mounted in a heavy yoke, is equipped with a counter-shaft provided with an automatic belt tightener. A 7-inch belt is used. This head may be tilted 30 degrees to the right and 20 degrees to the left and set in an exact position by means of a graduated scale. Most of the bevels used in wooden shipbuilding do not exceed 10 degrees. The side head is fitted with an adjustable guiding collar, which governs the depth of the cut.

Displays Remarkable Efficiency

The 48-inch top-beveling head may be tilted 15 degrees either way. It also may be raised or lowered by power and set by means of a dial that shows thicknesses to sixty-fourths. The roller table, or traveling bed, is 80 feet long. When motor-driven, a 50-horsepower motor is required. When working ceiling and planking, it is said the machine will replace 18 carpenters on the skids, the net labor saving alone amounting to over $85 per day.

After the keelson timbers and ceiling strakes are beveled, they usually are hauled up inside the ship through a chute similar to that shown in Fig. 131. An ordinary hoisting engine and 1/2 or 5/8-inch wire rope is used for this operation. After the keelsons and ceiling are in place, the hole left in the frames for the chute is filled up.

When the keelson timbers reach their proper position inside the hull, they are first clamped down, as shown in Fig. 137, using clamps similar to those illustrated in Fig. 145. After they are clamped in place, the timbers are drift-bolted to the floor, as shown in Figs. 139 and 140. The drift-bolts are 1 to 1¼ inches in diameter and from 24 to 30 inches in length; usually

they are set by means of pneumatic hammers.

Three steps in the construction of a center girder-keelson in a 290-foot motor schooner at the plant of the Grays Harbor Ship Building Co., Aberdeen, Wash., are shown in Figs. 144, 146 and 147. This center girder consists of eight 12 x 18-inch keelsons laid on top of the rider keelson. As shown in Fig. 147, the keelsons form an arch extending up to the height of the hold beams amidship and tapering down on both ends. The various sections of the keelsons are skidded into place and clamped by means of chains and wedges, as shown in Fig. 146. As soon as this is done, the holes are bored for the edge-bolts, using a pneumatic auger. The bolts are then driven and the chain clamps removed. Afterwards the timber runway, shown in Fig. 147, is taken down.

Before the ceiling or inner planking can be bolted in place, the frames must be dubbed-off to a fair surface, as shown in Fig. 150. This operation is performed by adzes, skilled men being necessary. To facilitate the dubbing-off process a temporary scaffolding is built around the sides of the vessel, as shown in Fig. 150. Two different methods of laying the ceiling are shown in Figs. 132 and 149. In the latter case, in a southern shipyard, the ceiling is laid from the keelson out to the bilge in parallel strakes. In the ship shown in Fig. 132, the bilge ceiling is first bolted in place and then the semielliptical space between the lower edge of the bilge ceiling and the keelson is filled in. The latter method generally is considered the more satisfactory, producing a stronger ship. Fig. 132 also shows the arrangement of the scaffolding for fastening the ceiling strakes to the upper part of the inside ship.

Fig. 152 shows how the ceiling near the main deck is clamped and bolted in place. It will be noted that a temporary scaffolding supported by horses is used. This illustration shows the general nature of the clamps employed for temporarily fastening ceiling strakes.

Another view of the ceiling operation, near the stern, is show in Fig. 153. This illustration shows clearly how the ceiling is clamped in place before being drift-bolted. It also indicates how the ends of the ceiling are beveled against the stern post and after-end of the keelson.

New Wooden Vessels Vie With Steel

In all corners of the country, the carpenter and the riveter are matching their skill against the German. The steel tanker above was built at Camden, N. J., the steel bulk freighter below at Detroit. The larger wooden boats were built at Portland, Oreg., the one in the small inset, at Millbridge, Me.

CHAPTER IX

Construction of Hold Bracing and Deck Elements

WOODEN ships are held together internally by various combinations of timbers, the most important of which are the beams which connect the upper ends of the frames. These beams are covered by deck planking and usually they are supported in the middle by posts or stanchions. In large ships, two rows of beams are inserted, known respectively as hold beams and main deck beams. The ends of the beams are secured either by wooden or steel knees or by a shelf and clamp construction, the details of which will be described later. There is some doubt among modern shipbuilders of the efficiency of beams for tying the upper parts of the ship together and resisting twisting strains. It is pointed out that the nature of the connection between the beam's ends and the sides of the vessel is such that the beams should be considered as supported and not fixed. In order to give the deck construction more strength, therefore, most modern ship builders resort to the use of longitudinal or diagonal steel straps. The former usually extend right fore and aft under the waterways and alongside the hatches. Where diagonal straps also are employed, they are arranged in the shape of a lattice or simple truss between the hatchways.

The necessity for hold stanchions or posts is evident from a consideration of the strains to which the ship is subjected when empty. In such a case, the bottom must resist the enormous upward push of the water and as stated in one of the earlier chapters in this book, many wooden vessels have been found insufficiently strong to resist these forces, with the result that the bottom has caved upward. This has occurred even where hold stanchions are provided in the ordinary manner. In such cases, however, the bulging is not nearly as great as it would be if there were no stanchions. When, on account of weak floors, such bulging occurs with the stanchions in place, the deck beams are lifted up at the center and the round of beams is exaggerated.

Contrasting Methods

Two contrasting methods of framing hold stanchions are shown in Figs. 154 and 155, and 156 and 157, respectively. In the former case, the stanchions, which are of relatively light cross-section, are arranged in pairs. These pairs face athwartship in the way of the hatches and longitudinally between the hatches. A detail of the stanchion footings is shown in Fig. 154, which indicates how the lower ends of the stanchions fit onto

the wide, flat keelsons. It will be noted that a hardwood block is provided to take the thrust and that the footing is further reinforced by short sections of angle iron. The details and dimensions of this framing are given in Fig. 40, page 27, in the fourth chapter of this book.

A more conventional type of hold framing is shown in Figs. 156 and 157. This illustrates the framing of a 290-foot, 5-masted auxiliary schooner which is provided with both hold and main deck beams. It is readily apparent that there is a more lavish use of timber than in the design shown in Figs. 154 and 155. The stanchions shown in Fig. 157 are divided into two section by the hold beams. The lower section foots on the center girder-keelson. The stringers, or caps, carrying the deck beams are shown clearly in

FIG. 154—DETAIL OF STANCHION FOOTINGS IN A LARGE WOODEN SHIP.   FIG. 155—GENERAL VIEW OF STANCHIONS IN THE SAME SHIP

FIG. 156—STANCHIONS BETWEEN MAIN AND LOWER DECK BEAMS. FIG. 157—GENERAL VIEW OF HOLD FRAMING
FIG. 158—SAFETY LADDER INSIDE SHIP. FIG. 159—DUBBING-OFF STERN BULWARKS

FIG. 160—ARRANGEMENT OF DECK BEAMS NEAR STERN.   FIG. 161—DECK OF WOODEN MOTOR SCHOONER NEARLY COMPLETED

Fig. 156. Further details and dimensions of this framing may be obtained by referring to Fig. 36, page 24, published in the fourth chapter of this book.

Incidentally, it might be stated that many wooden ship builders fail to appreciate the necessity for providing safe entrances and exits to their vessels during construction. Scaffolding and ladders of the flimsiest character are often considered sufficient. As a result, accidents have been abnormally high in wooden shipyards. The resulting loss may be readily avoided by giving a little thought to the subject of safety. Fig. 158 shows how one ship builder in Portland, Oreg., solved the problem of providing a safe entrance to the hold by building a cheap, strong plank stairway which was properly protected by rope rails.

Two different forms of deck beam construction are shown in Figs. 164 and 165, and 162 and 163, respectively. In either case, the ends of the deck beams rest on a line of timbers secured to the inside surface of the frames. This combination of timbers is termed a shelf. In some cases, however, the topmost timber only, which carries the direct weight of the beams, is called the shelf, the timbers immediately underneath being known as clamps. The shelf is fastened with bolts, as shown in Fig. 164; ordinary drift bolts clenched on the inside usually are employed, although in some cases, as in Fig. 162, through bolts provided with nuts and washers are used instead.

In the construction shown in Fig. 164, which is the more usual type, the ends of the shelf or clamp timbers

are simply butted together. In the vessel shown in Fig. 162, these timbers are scarfed at the joints. Considerable difference of opinion exists with reference to the utility of scarfing the various lengths of timber composing the shelf. Some builders advocate the necessity of so doing on the ground that the greater the number of plain butts in the length of the ship, the less the resistance offered to such changes of form as sagging and hogging. It is claimed that by preserving as far as possible continuity of strength in the shelf, the ship is materially aided in resisting strains. This has been urged more especially in the case of large ships. On the other hand, it has been maintained that the scarfing of a single course or so of longitudinal timbers can afford but little additional

FIG. 162—DECK BEAMS RESTING ON SHELF, BOLTED CONSTRUCTION.   FIG. 163—DETAILS OF FASTENINGS OF SHELF AND CLAMP

FIG. 164—MAIN-DECK BEAMS WITH HANGING KNEES IN PLACE.   FIG. 165—MAIN DECK BEAMS FITTED TO SHELF.   FIG. 166— SPIKING DOWN DECK PLANKING.
FIG. 167—CLAMPING DECK PLANKING IN PLACE

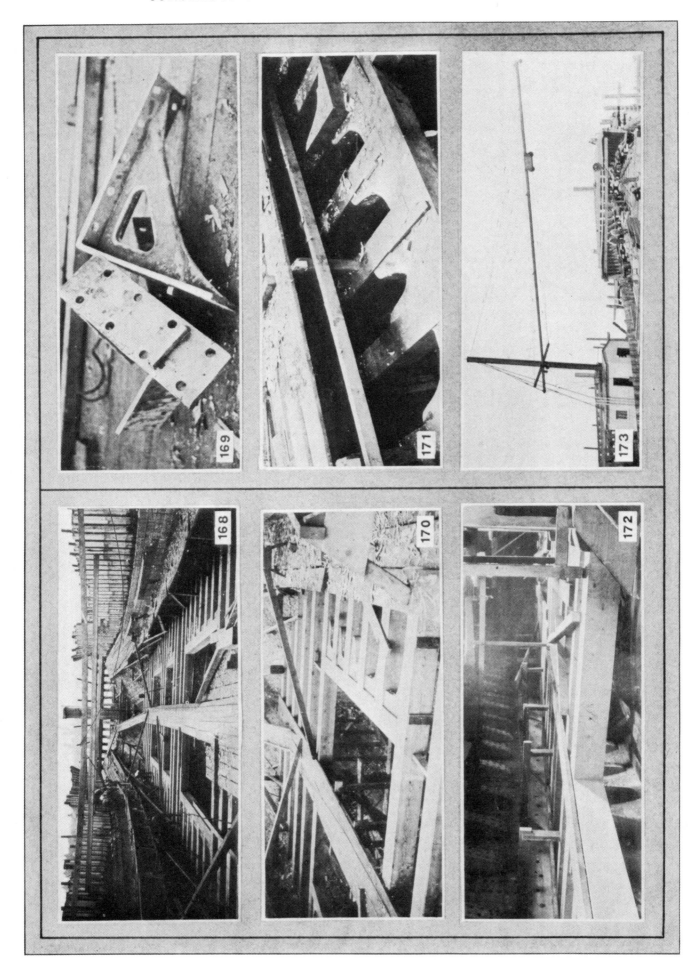

FIG. 168—GENERAL VIEW OF HOLD BEAMS SHOWING LUMBER CHUTE. FIG. 169—DETAIL OF CAST STEEL KNEES. FIG. 170—HOLD BEAMS IN THE WAY OF A HATCH. FIG. 171—LODGING KNEES IN THE WAY OF A HATCH. FIG. 172—DETAIL OF HATCH BEAM CONSTRUCTION. FIG. 173—CRANE USED FOR SETTING DECK BEAMS

FIG. 174—SURFACING KNEES ON A SPECIAL PLANING MACHINE—KNEES ALSO ARE FAYED ON THIS MACHINE
IN LOTS OF 10 OR 12, THE OPERATION REQUIRING ONLY 15 MINUTES

support and that the benefits derived are not proportionate to the expense involved. There is no doubt, however, that the scarfed joint is the stronger of the two.

As soon as the shelf is in place, the exterior planks opposite it may be trimmed and fitted. When this is done, the whole constitutes a very rigid ribband which preserves the form of the ship while the remainder of the plank is put on. Usually the beam knees are not fitted until some considerable time after the shelf is put in place.

Lloyd's rules require that for ships whose length is five times their breadth, and between eight and nine times their depth, the sectional areas of shelves and waterways shall not be

less than that of the beams, the latter being determined by a table giving the scantlings according to the breadth of the ship amidships. The rules also require that the breadths of the faying surfaces of such shelves shall not be less than the siding given for the beam. When the fastenings are of iron, they need not go through the exterior planks, but may be clenched either on the inside of the shelf or outside of the timbers. If copper or yellow metal fastenings are used for any purpose, they must be clenched on the outer planks.

Beams Perform Two-Fold Service

As previously suggested, the beams perform the two-fold service of connecting the sides of the ship and of

forming the foundation for the decks which carry out the internal economy of the vessel. Besides this, the beams, in combination with the deck planks form a continuation of the frames and planking, it being evident that when the ship is rolling and working heavily in a seaway, the deck and beams at intervals are subjected to the same strains as the frames and the outside planking.

Usually, the framing of a wooden deck consists of beams, half beams and carlings. The beams are those which extend continuously from one side to the other. Half beams are short beams of reduced scantling which extend from the side to fore and aft pieces of deck framing termed carlings. The latter are fitted between

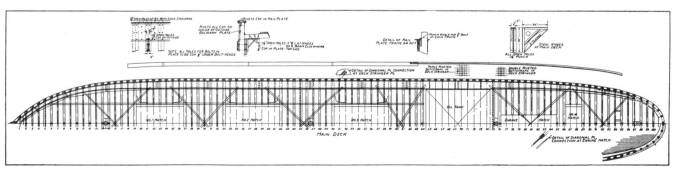

FIG. 175—SECTION OF DECK FRAMING OF LARGE WOODEN SHIP SHOWING METHOD OF REINFORCING WITH STEEL
PLATES AND STRAPS

the beams. The arrangement of the deck framing is given in the design of the ship and is adapted to the required position of the hatchways, companionways, etc. The beams are cut with parallel siding and molding, the upper surface being formed to the curvature of a circular arch. The versed sine of this arch is termed the round-up of the beam. This curvature prevents the water from lodging on the deck and adds to the bearing power of the beam when its ends are fixed.

In modern yards the beams usually are trimmed on a band saw or edging machine. For this purpose, beam molds or tables of dimensions are provided. The molds may be prepared in the mold loft in the following manner:

The line of the beam at middle is rased or scratched in on the floor in the body plan, being copied into that plan from the sheer plan by measuring square to the base line the height at which the beam at middle line in sheer cuts each square station, transferring these heights to the body plan square to the base line. The midship beam itself also is drawn in the body plan, being copied from the midship section. The distance between the beam end and the beam middle lines at any square station in the sheer plan is evidently the round-up in the length of the beam. Therefore, having given the latter line, together with

the curve of the longest beam and the length of the beams in the deck under consideration, the former line is at once determined by setting the

FIG. 176—DECK OF LARGE WOODEN MOTOR SCHOONER

amount of round-up for the beam at each square station below the latter, passing a curve through the points so obtained. The curve of the beam itself is that of an arc of a circle.

Since this circle is necessarily of very large radius, the portion of it that is required may be most conveniently constructed by certain simple methods explained in most works on plane geometry or mechanical drawing.

After the inside of the ship has been dubbed-out fair, it is a good idea to rase in the line for the beams on the ship's side. The first operation in getting in a line of a tier of beams is that of marking a straight line on the ship's side at or near the height of the beam at middle line amidships. The straight line is drawn first on the sheer draft and its height is measured from the keel. Three boards are then put across from side to side, one being near each extremity of the ship and one at the middle. These boards should be set perfectly horizontal by means of a spirit level and they are so placed that the upper edges of the two extreme boards are at the height of the straight line, and out of winding with the lower edge of the middle board. This is done by looking across the edges or sighting as it is termed. Battens then are fixed along the inside of the ship. The end batten is so placed that its upper edge coincides with the upper edges of the two extreme base boards and the lower edge of the middle board. The intermediate portions of the upper edges of the battens are looked level with the three edges of the baseboards, and the straight line

FIG. 177—CAULKING DECK USING HEAVY MAUL.   FIG. 178— FINISH CAULKING.   FIG. 179—INSERTING PINE PLUGS OVER SPIKEHEADS IN DECK

is thus sighted on the inside surface of the frames. This line is then rased in on the timbers, after which it may be painted so as to be readily distinguishable. In this way a straight line may be put in on both sides of the ship at the same height above the keel.

Next, the perpendicular distance between the straight line and the beam at middle line in the sheer draft is measured at every square station or frame station. A small cord is now set to cross the ship at each square station, being kept to the straight lines already drawn on each side of the ship. In this position a spirit level is sometimes applied to the cord to prove the agreement of the straight lines on the ship's side. The distances measured from the drawing are then set up from the cord, square to the base line, at the respective square stations, and the points so found are marked on the inside surface of the timbers on both sides of the ship. A line drawn to all the points by aid of sheering battens, gives the sheer of the deck or the projection of the beams at middle upon the sides of the timbers.

Marking in the Lines

The beams at side line, that is the line of the upper side of the beam ends, is then found by measuring from the beam mold the round down of the beam in the breadth of the ship at each square station, and this distance is set down square from the line of the beams at middle. The spots so found are marked on the timbers. A line drawn through all such points, by the aid of sheering battens, is the line of the beams at side. It is evident that by setting beneath this line, the molding of the beam, minus the snaping of the end, we obtain points in the line of the upper edge of the shelf, which line can then be drawn by the aid of sheering battens.

For trimming the shelf, molds may be made to the curvature of the side and the amount of sheer determined by spilings taken from a straight line drawn on the inside of the timbers, adjacent to the line of shelf, for the length of the piece to be trimmed. These spilings are set off from a corresponding straight line drawn on the timber when trimming it.

The correct section of the shelf amidships is given in the design and the shelf is kept the same siding and molding throughout its entire length. The upper side usually slopes slightly inward and the under side is more frequently parallel to the under side of the beam than square to the surface of the timbers. At the extremities of the ship, the shelf usually is tapered away to the thickness of the clamps or ceiling.

Two types of knees, wood and steel, respectively, are shown in Figs. 164 and 169. Knees may be either hanging or lodging, that is, vertical or horizontal, as shown respectively in Figs. 165 and 170. The chief function of knees at beam ends is to preserve a constant angle between the beam and the ship's side, it being evident that the working of a ship in a seaway tends to alter that angle. Considerable difference of opinion exists regarding the relative efficiency of natural-bent wood knees, such as shown in Fig. 165 and the cast steel knees illustrated in Fig. 169. The latter are about 4 feet 6 inches on a side and ⅞ inch in section. They are, of course, much stiffer than the wood knees; they also are lighter and less unsightly. It is claimed by some builders, however, that their very stiffness is undesirable. it being the contention of these shipwrights that all parts of the ship's structure should work together. On the Pacific coast, natural wood knees can be obtained in almost any size, with arms up to 8 or 10 feet length and thicknesses up to 24 inches. In some cases, the clamp and shelf construction is so arranged that the use of hanging knees under the beams is obviated.

The length of a wooden beam usually is measured at the tip. This can be done either by measuring the breadth of the ship straight across, at the level of the upper edge of the beam, then applying this length to the beam mold, and measuring the length of the curved edge of the mold in the straight distance, or it can be done by putting the beam mold in place and marking-off the length on it. By the latter method the beveling of the beam ends, if any, can be marked on the mold at the same time.

To Take the Snape of a Beam

In order to take account of the snape of the beam end. also of the beveling and length at one time. whether the beam is at its correct round or not, the following is an ordinary method:

A batten is placed across the ship at the position of the beam to be fitted, and the upper edge is kept in touch with a cord stretched tightly across the ship and secured to the beam end line at each extremity. A piece of mold is then made to the shape of each of the beam ends. These molds are nailed to the ends of the batten. while the latter is in the position already named. The battens with the end molds are then laid upon the beam to be cut. The ends may now be marked by the molds and in order to be sure that the beam fits closely against the timbers, it is customary to allow an extra length of say ¼ to ¾ inch, in proportion to the length of the beam, the exact amount being regulated by a slip of wood kept by the workman who thereby makes it certain that all of the beams are wedged in equally. The fore and aft bevelings of the beam ends, if any, are taken with a bevel held against an athwartship line and the inside of the timbers. It is of the utmost importance that the beams should fit closely against the frame timbers. A close joint is popularly said to be half the fastening and nowhere is this more true than in the case of beams.

Steel Tape May Be Used

In a good many American shipyards where speed is the chief consideration, these precautions to insure correctly fitted beams frequently are omitted, simple measurements with a steel tape taking their place. Very often this does quite well, but if a well-built ship is desired, too much care cannot be taken in fitting its parts together.

After the beams are laid and prior to planking the deck, it is necessary to arrange for the deck furnishings. These fittings consist of hatchways, scuttles, match partners, bitts, bollards, capstans, etc. The sides of the hatchways are formed with carlings which are scored into the beams. Coamings and headledges are bolted above the carlings, the former being placed in a fore and aft, the latter in a transverse or athwartship direction. They are referred to by the general name of coamings, and extend to a sufficient height above the deck plank to prevent water from getting through the hatchway under ordinary conditions.

The mast holes of a ship with wood beams are framed with a series of carlings termed fore-and-aft partners, cross-partners and angle-chocks, the whole forming a hole the diameter of which exceeds that of the section of the mast usually by twice the thickness of the mast wedges. The latter vary from about 3 inches to 6 inches, according to the size of the ship. The framings for capstans, bollards, riding bitts, etc., are built up simply of carlings fitted so as to form a solid resting place or bearing for the fitting in question.

The deck planking for American wooden ships of normal size usually consists of 5-inch square, edge-grain fir or yellow pine timbers laid longitudinally, as shown in Figs. 166 and 167. The latter illustration shows how the deck planks are clamped and wedged into place before being spiked down. Fig. 166 shows the method of

spiking down the short lengths of plank between hatchways. Ten-inch galvanized boat spikes usually are employed. They may be driven with an air hammer instead of by hand.

Great care should be taken in laying the deck plank as it presents a very unsightly appearance when irregularly or carelessly put down. The edges should be fair, but not necessarily straight, as it sometimes is considered advisable to taper the strakes toward the bow in a curvilinear manner in order to neutralize the optical illusion of curved deck edges which is produced by parallel straight seams approaching a side of considerable curvature. In most American ships, the deck planks are straight and parallel. Whether straight or curved, it is absolutely necessary that the edges be fair. If the practice shown in Fig. 167 of laying several strakes together is followed very fair and even seams may be obtained.

The heads of the deck spikes are countersunk and the holes are filled with soft, white-pine plugs laid in white lead. The method of performing this operation is shown clearly in Fig. 179. After the spike heads are plugged, the deck is caulked. The preliminary caulking is performed by two men, as shown in Fig. 177. One holds the caulking iron and the other swings the maul. The final caulking is performed by one man who sits on a campstool and uses a light mallet. This operation is shown in Fig. 178. Fig. 176 shows the finished deck of a 5-masted wooden auxiliary schooner.

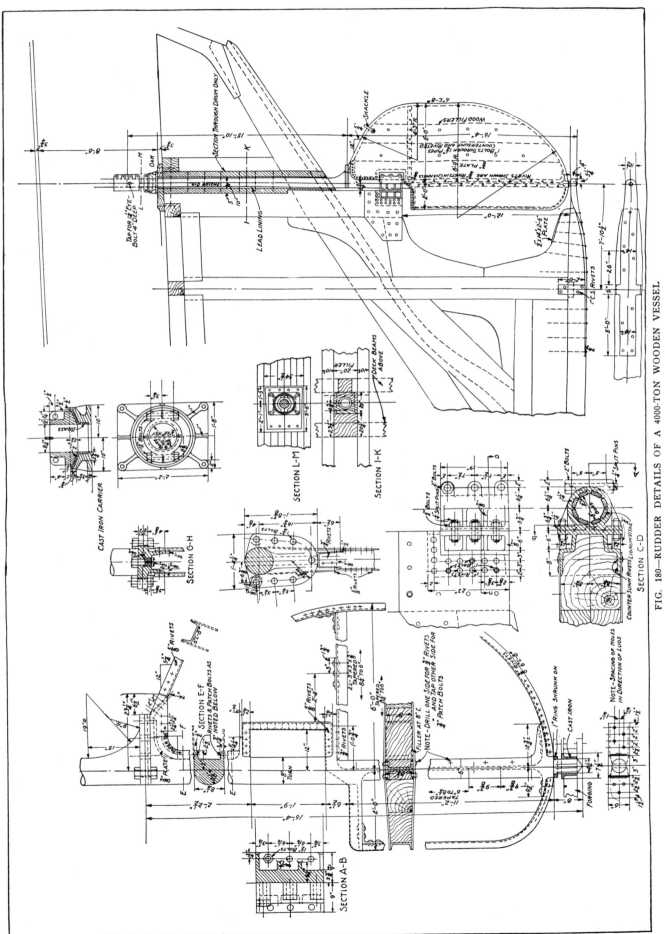

FIG. 180—RUDDER DETAILS OF A 4000-TON WOODEN VESSEL

CHAPTER X

Spars, Rudders, Shaft Logs and Engine Beds

SOME wooden shipbuilders make their own spars; others purchase them from spar specialists. Most of the timber for spars comes from the Pacific northwest on account of the abundance of tall, straight trees free from limbs close to the ground, obtainable in that section of the country. Up-to-date machinery has been employed very little in working-up spars. Skilled men, therefore, are necessary. Figs. 185 and 187 show the essential operations in preparing a spar or mast. For convenience in handling, the rough logs usually are laid on timbers which raise them about 2 feet from the ground. When the shipyard works up its own spars, the logs are purchased peeled. In order to obtain the proper taper, it is first necessary to rough-out the spar with an adz or axe, as shown in Fig. 185. This is a rather laborious and tiresome operation which at the same time must be carefully conducted. After the spar is roughed-out it is planed to a true surface by means of hand planes of various sizes as shown in Fig. 187. Sometimes spars are scraped and sandpapered. Generally, also, they are varnished before being set in place.

Some wooden shipbuilders are now using steel masts which are lighter than wood, and in some sections of the country more readily obtainable. In the case of an auxiliary vessel, the steel mast also has an advantage, in that it may be employed as an exhaust pipe for the engine.

It hardly need be stated that a rudder is necessary to govern the direction of the ship's motion through the water, the operation involved being termed steering. The rudder, therefore, is a very important part of the ship. Fig. 184 shows a wood rudder of standard type for a large wooden auxiliary vessel. Another type of rudder also used on wooden ships is shown in Fig. 180. This rudder is of the composite type with a cast steel frame and wood filling.

How the Rudder Stock is Coned

Referring now to Fig. 184, it will be seen that a line drawn through the center of a rudder pintles coincides with the center line of the rudder stock. Fig. 184 shows clearly how this result is obtained in the case of a wooden rudder, the lower end of the rudder stock, known as the coning, being trimmed or coned to fit a corresponding cavity in the rudder.

Formerly, the fore-side of the rudder was straight, and therefore the center line of pintles, about which the rudder revolves, was at a distance about equal to the radius of the pintles from the fore-side of the rudder stock. It is evident that a large hole was necessary under these circumstances to permit the rudder to turn through the required angle. The difficulty of making this hole watertight, leather being usually employed, led to the construction shown in Fig. 184.

The rudder itself is built of pieces of timber rigidly edge-bolted together. The after side is protected by an iron strap or forging. Hardwood invariably is employed, iron bark, a dense hard wood obtained from Australia usually being used in the United States. The rudder pintles, usually four in number, are generally bronze castings. They fit into bronze sockets bolted to the rudder post. Complete details of this construction are shown in Fig. 117, in the seventh chapter. Further details of wooden rudder construction may be obtained by referring to Figs. 102 and 104 in the same chapter.

As Figs. 102 and 117 clearly indicate, the after portion of the rudderpost or sternpost, as the case may

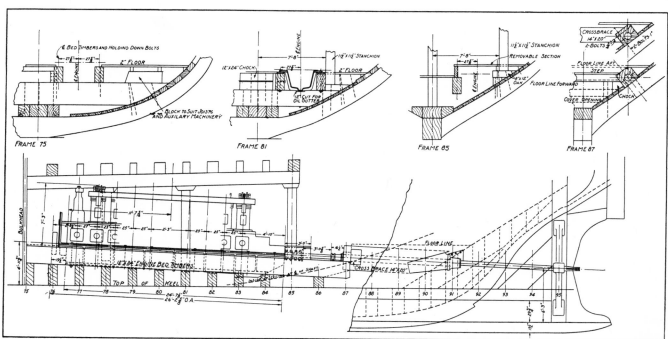

FIG. 181—FOUNDATION DETAILS FOR A TWIN-SCREW OIL-ENGINE DRIVEN SHIP FITTED WITH 500-HORSEPOWER, 6-CYLINDER ENGINES

FIG. 182—IRON-BARK RUDDER STOCK SET UP ON TRAVELING TABLE OF BEVELING MACHINE

be, is trimmed or beveled, similarly to the forepart of the rudder shown in Fig. 184, in order to allow the rudder to turn through the requisite angle. This trimming which is known as bearding, is usually sufficient to permit the rudder to turn about 45 degrees each way, as the angle of maximum efficiency is just within these limits.

The method of setting-off the bearding is worthy of description. Although the line through the centers of the pintles is the axis of rotation, the sides of the bearded portion of the rudder do not radiate from this line but from the fore sides of the pintles. This is done in order that the bearings on the rudderpost may be placed further aft, thus reducing the amount of wood which must be cut out for the boss to work in. This is especially desirable at the lower end of the post, which in some cases would be cut off to a sliver edge on each side if it were bearded from the center of the pintles.

Machinery Employed

Formerly all of the operations connected with making a rudder were performed by hand. At the present time machinery is employed for surfacing the various pieces as well as for working up the rudder stock itself.

Figs. 182 and 183 show how heavy iron-bark rudder stocks may be formed on a special shipbuilders' planing, edging and beveling machine. This machine, which has been previously described, is provided with a traveling table for handling timbers. Fig. 183 shows how the stock is placed on chocks sawed to hold it at 45 degrees. After the stock is blocked up in this manner, it is run through the machine and the cutting is done by the top beveling head. Inasmuch as

the wood is especially hard, comparatively light cuts are taken and each time the carriage is reversed the top beveling head is lowered slightly

FIG. 185—ROUGHING OUT A SPAR WITH AN AXE

by power. This head is provided with a dial indicator which shows its exact position. This operation is continued until the cut is brought down to the desired depth. The rudder stock is then turned so that another corner can be cut down to the same depth in the same manner. By continuing this operation, the stock can be reduced in the machine from the rough to practically a finished condition.

The rudder shown in Fig. 180 is of the balanced type. It extends 6 feet abaft the pintles and 2 feet in front of them. This rudder has an overall height of 16 feet 4 inches. It is supported at the lower end by a cast steel shoe. The rudder stock

is a forged steel shaft turned to a diameter of 8 inches. The pintle bearing at the lower end is turned to a diameter of 4¼ inches. The rudder sleeve is lined with lead. The inside diameter of the sleeve is 10 inches and the walls are 5 inches in thickness.

In preparing the engine foundations for wooden ships, the methods vary considerably among different shipyards. The object of the builder in each case is to furnish a firm foundation which will hold the engine securely and keep the shaft in alignment. In wooden vessels, particularly where the machinery is amidships, this question of shaft alignment is a serious one owing to the twisting of the hull in service. In order to avoid the troubles which result from this displacement of the hull, some builders of oil engines recommend the use of flexible couplings of the usual pin and leather-ring type. Some of these builders also place the engines parallel to the propeller shaft, in the case of twin screw boats, transmitting the power through a herringbone gear. This is said to permit the engine to run at a more economical speed.

Solid Foundation

Some builders of motor ships prefer to place their engines on a foundation built of solid 12 x 12-inch timbers. They believe this is necessary in order to fortify the structure against the shocks of pre-ignition. Experience has shown, however, that in the case of well designed engines this is not necessary. A type of foundation for a 6-cylinder 500-horsepower oil engine, which is much more economical of timber than the solid block type is illustrated in Fig. 181. This drawing shows very clearly the various details of the foundation.

In this case, the engine is carried on two 12 x 24-inch continuous foundation timbers. The engine is approximately 26 feet in length over all.

FIG. 187—FINISHING A SPAR WITH A HAND PLANE

Fig. 181 also shows one arrangement of shaft log and stern tube. Two types of stern tubes are in general use. In one design, for twin-screw motor vessels, the propeller shaft is carried through a built-up wood shaft log, about 28 inches square on the outside. Sometimes the log is built out of two pieces with a single longitudinal parting. In other cases, four pieces thoroughly edge-bolted together are employed. The log is rabbeted into the planking and ceiling, and caulked tight. It is provided with a lead sleeve and with cast iron caps on each end.

The other design involves the use of a cast-steel sleeve or stern tube

FIG. 186—STEAM-DRIVEN CARGO WINCH INSTALLED ON WOODEN SHIP. FIG. 188—STEAM-DRIVEN ANCHOR WINCH BUILT ON PACIFIC COAST

with bronze liners at each end carrying lignum vitae bushings. The shaft between the bushings is served with marlin. The shaft bearings are bored out to their proper alignment after the log is in place, using a portable electric-driven boring machine. The boring machine usually is driven by a 7½-horsepower motor connected to the boring-bar through a worm gear.

The cost of installing an oil engine in a modern motor ship varies considerably depending on the size of the vessel and the skill of the installing foreman. Generally speaking, it ought not to cost over $3000 to install two 350-horsepower semidiesel outfits complete with tanks. The job should be accomplished in from 13 to 20 days. Some shipbuilders, however, have spent as much as $7000 installing two engines, and in one case, at least, fully two months' time was required.

The deck fittings for wooden ships do not differ materially from those employed on steel vessels. Fig. 186 shows a typical cargo hoist and Fig. 188 an anchor winch installed on a 5-masted auxiliary schooner. Both of these machines are steam driven. Electrically driven winches also are used to a considerable extent, particularly on power driven vessels where it may not be convenient to provide steam. On motor ships, horizontal oil or coal fired donkey boilers with some 480 to 700 square feet of heating surface usually are provided. In some cases, larger boilers have been found advisable, with up to 1000 square feet of heating surface.

Wood vessels are launched in the same manner as steel ships. On the coast or wherever end launching is employed, a cradle is built under both ends of the vessel. This cradle, of course, rests on the standing ways. When the ship is ready for launching, it is raised off the keel blocks by wedges. Then the shores and keel blocks are knocked out transferring the weight of the ship to the cradle. In some cases the sliding ways are spiked to the standing ways to hold the ship prior to launching. In this case, the ways are sawed apart by two men at the moment of launching. In other cases the usual trigger gear is employed. On the Great Lakes, vessels are launched sideways. The general principles are similar, the ways running athwartship instead of longitudinally.

Vessels usually are painted above the waterline as well as below before launching. In some yards the paint is sprayed on by a pneumatic atomizer. This device saves considerable time and makes it easy for an unskilled man to produce a smooth coat. A large ship will require from 70,000 to 100,000 pounds of paint. In some yards sailing vessels are launched with the masts and most of the rigging in place. In other establishments the hull is sent into the water without any rigging.

How Wooden Ships Are Laid Off

By SAMUEL J. P. THEARLE

Supplement to How Wooden Ships Are Built

CHAPTER I

Fundamental Propositions

LAYING down or laying off is the name given to that art by the aid of which the shipbuilder determines the forms of the various pieces of which a ship's hull is composed, so that when they are put together in their proper positions, they shall collectively constitute the frame of a ship, having the form and dimensions intended by the designer. It is sometimes styled the geometry of shipbuilding, and is, in fact, a practical application of descriptive geometry to that art. Its various problems are solved upon the floor of a building known as the mold loft, where the drawings furnished by the designer are transferred in chalk lines in full size, and then by the aid of geometry, and in the manner discussed in the following paragraphs,, the draftsman determines and draws in the shapes of the various components of the frame. Molds or patterns are made to the lines, and with them and other data furnished by the draftsman, the workmen are enabled to trim the timbers, or bend the angle-irons, and place such marks upon them as shall leave nothing but the putting together and fastening them in their places in order to construct the frame of the ship.

The application of geometry to shipbuilding has now become almost universal. In some small yards, however, schooners, brigs, and such minor craft, are not laid off; but the stem, sternposts, and the keel having been set in position, the form of the hull is shaped in on one side with battens bent to please the eye; and molds having been made to the timbers on that side, they are reversed for the timbers on the other side. The timbers are kept in place by cross spalls, shores, and ribbands, the frame is planked, and thus the hull is built. Although this mode is not very objectionable practically in vessels of such description that no special design is required, it could not be entertained for a moment in navy

yards or large private firms, where all ships are built from well matured designs that must be adhered to in their entirety; besides which, owing to the ships being of so large a size, this mocking system is economically impracticable.

A Difficult Art

To an ordinary observer, the determination of lines on a ship's surface presents itself as a series of problems of no little intricacy; and, indeed, were it not that all, or nearly all, such lines as the naval architect requires, are produced by plane intersections with the ship's surface, their determination, owing to the undevelopable nature of that surface, would be both approximate and difficult. To solve these problems is the province of laying off. A study of this subject will be greatly assisted by a previous perusal of any standard work on descriptive geometry; and a clear conception of certain of the more difficult problems of ship design will be found impossible without an acquaintance with that portion of descriptive geometry which treats of straight lines and planes.

Before proceeding with the practical operations in laying off, it is necessary to state and explain the following preliminary proposition:

A point in space is determined, or fully known, when its distances are given from three planes mutually at right angles.

Consider $AOCD$, $BOCF$, $AOBE$, Fig. 1, to be three sides of a square-cornered cubical box of unlimited dimensions; that is, let each of these plane surfaces extend indefinitely from OB, OC and OA. For the present, suppose $OBEA$ to be the bottom; then, if the perpendicular distances of a point in the bottom from the sides OB and OA be given, a mechanic with his rule and square will immediately find its position by measuring from the point O along OA, the given distance OX of

the point from the line OB, and also measuring from the point O along OB, the given distance OY of the point from the line OA; then by squaring out lines from the points X and Y, he knows that their intersection is the point P required. This action in the everyday life, of the skilled mechanic, is no other than that of determining a point whose co-ordinates. are given; the distances OX and OY being the co-ordinates. OB and OA are termed the axes.

But a ship being a solid and not a plane, another dimension must be introduced before the required point can be determined, namely, height or depth; hitherto only length and breadth have been considered. Returning to Fig. 1, it is seen that if a line be drawn through the point P perpendicular to the plane $OBEA$, or, which is the same thing, parallel to the line OC, there are any number of points in this line, each of which is distant PX and PY from the planes $AOCD$ and $BOCF$ respectively, but at any fixed distance from the plane $AOBE$. If, then, a height PQ be taken in this line, a point Q is found, which is distant PX, PY, and PQ from the planes $AOCD$, $BOCF$ and $AOBE$, respectively. Now there is only one point which fulfills these conditions, for only one perpendicular can be drawn through the point P, and there is only one point in that perpendicular which is distant PQ from the plane $AOBE$. Hence the point Q has been determined by having given its distances from three planes mutually at right angles.

The planes $AOCD$, $BOCF$ and $AOBE$ are termed in geometry planes of reference or co-ordinate planes, and have their laying off counterparts in the sheer, body and half-breadth plans, respectively.

As we have already stated, nearly all the lines on a ship's surface which are employed in laying off, are contained in planes; hence, they are drawn upon

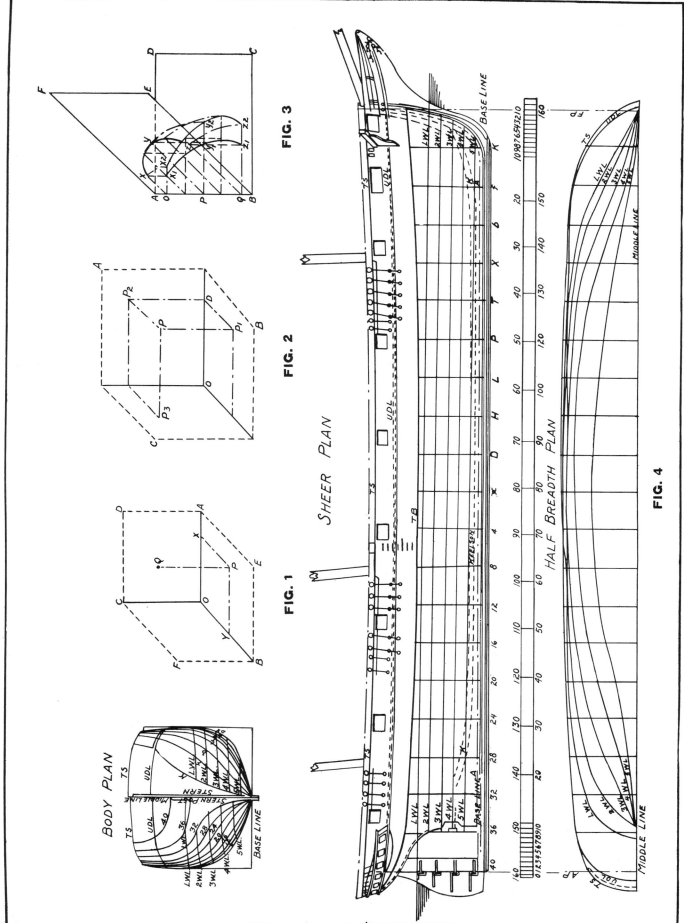

FIG. 1—PROJECTING A POINT ON A PLANE.   FIG. 2—DETERMINING A POINT IN SPACE.   FIG. 3—RABATTING A LINE.   FIG. 4—SHEER DRAFT OF A SLOOP OF WAR

a plane surface, and in order to have a correct conception of the forms of the lines, they are projected upon three planes of reference.

Definitions and Axioms

The projection of a line upon a plane is the foot of the perpendicular let fall from the point upon the plane.

The projection of a line upon a plane is the line which passes through the feet of all the perpendiculars which can be let fall from the line to the plane.

The plane upon which the perpendicular is let fall, is termed the plane of projection; and the perpendicular itself is known as the projecting line.

When a straight line is projected upon a plane, the plane containing the projected lines is termed the projecting plane.

When a line is in a plane parallel to the plane of projection, the projected length and form are the same as the true length and form of the line; but if the planes are not parallel, the projected line will not be similar to the real line; and the latter can then be determined by what is termed rabatting, to which we shall refer presently.

The intersections of lines with planes, and of planes with each other, are termed their traces; it is evident that the former are points and the latter straight lines.

The projections of all lines which are in a plane perpendicular to the plane of projection are straight lines, which evidently coincide with the trace of the former plane upon the latter.

When a line is perpendicular to the plane of projection, its projection will be the trace of the line produced to meet the plane.

The projections of a point upon two of the planes of reference, are all that is required to determine the point without the aid of the third plane. For, referring to Fig. 2, let P_1 be the horizontal, and P_2 and P_3 the two vertical projections of the point P; it is seen that in each of the planes OA and OB, two dimensions enter, length and depth in OA, represented by OD and P_2D respectively; and length and breadth in OB, represented by OD and P_1D respectively. Hence, if only these two plans are given, the three dimensions required, length, breadth and depth, are known, which are sufficient to determine the point. The projection of the point P on the plane OC at P_3, gives the dimensions breadth and depth; and as these are already known, the projection on that plane is not essential to a knowledge of the point when the projections on the other two planes are given. It is thus seen, that for the representation of the form of the vessel by the method of projections, it is

only necessary to have two of the three planes of reference; the three are, however, retained in order to give a clearer conception of the body projected, and for corroborative evidence; besides which, each of the plans contains lines which cannot be shown in their true shape in either of the others.

What Rabatting Is

It frequently happens that a line is in a plane which is not parallel to either of the planes of projection, and hence its projections do not show its true form. In order to obtain the latter, an operation termed rabatting is performed. It consists in hinging the plane containing the line about its trace with the plane which it is required to represent the line, or with a plane parallel to the last mentioned plane. In the first case, rabatment gives the line at once, and in the second case it has to be projected after being rabatted.

As an example of how a line is so rabatted, consider the following. In Fig. 3 let AB be the line of intersection of the two planes $ABCD$, $ABEF$, also, let xyz be a line in the latter plane which is required to represent in the former. It is evident that the projection $x_1y_1z_1$ of the line is not its real shape, the planes not being parallel; it is therefore necessary to rabat or hinge the plane $ABEF$ about AB, until it coincides with the plane $ABCD$. From any points, x, y, z, in the line xyz, draw xO, yP, and zQ, in the plane $ABEF$ perpendicular to AB; and from the points O, P, Q, draw in the plane $ABCD$ the straight lines Ox_2, Py_2, Qz_2, perpendicular to AB. Then take $Ox_2 = Ox$, $Py_2 = Py$, and $Qz_2 = Qz$; through the points x_2, y_2, z_2, draw the line x_2, y_2, z_2, and if the number of points x, y, z, taken are sufficient, the line $x_2y_2z_2$ will be the same as the line xyz.

Having thus briefly, and as simply as possible, stated the geometrical principles upon which the art of laying off is founded, and by which it is practiced, we will proceed to examine the manner of applying these principles and their equivalents in the art itself.

The Three Planes Explained

The three planes of reference are termed the body sheer, and half-breadth planes; they are the transverse vertical, longitudinal vertical and the horizontal planes respectively. The various lines which are projected upon these planes constitute the body, sheer and half-breadth plans. In the body plan, all such lines as in planes parallel to the horizontal plane, or perpendicular to the transverse vertical plane, will appear straight, as they are the traces of the last-mentioned plane with the planes

containing the lines. Those in the sheer plan, or perpendicular to the longitudinal vertical plane, will appear straight, for they are the traces of the longitudinal vertical or sheer plane with the planes containing the lines. Similar remarks apply to the half-breadth plan. In the body plan lines appear in their true form if the planes containing them are parallel to the transverse vertical or body plane; and similarly with regard to the other plans.

Planes of Intersection

For the purpose of representing the form of a ship upon plane surfaces and laying her off, she is supposed to be cut by three sets of planes parallel to the planes of reference. Three sets of lines are thus given by the intersection of these planes with the ship's surface, and their projections are termed level lines, buttock or bow lines, and square stations, according as they are produced by intersections of the surface with horizontal, longitudinal vertical and transverse vertical planes, respectively. The first appear straight in the body and sheer plans, but curved in half-breadth plan; the second are straight in the body and half-breadth, but curved in the sheer plan; and the third are straight in the sheer and half-breadth, but curved in the body.

By means of either two of these three sets of lines, having given two of the plans, the other plan may be drawn; or having given only one of the sets of lines in the three plans, and the projection of another set of lines on one of the three planes of reference, the projection of this set on each of the other planes of reference can be determined. All this readily follows from the principles of projection already explained.

Besides the preceding, other lines are introduced into the plans for special purposes to be named hereafter; of these the most important are diagonal lines. These are produced by the intersection of planes perpendicular to the body plane, but inclined to each of the other planes of reference; their horizontal projections are termed horizontal ribband lines, but the lines themselves are known as diagonal lines. By cutting the ship's surface more perpendicularly than those before mentioned, the diagonal planes give better intersections, and are thus of great service in "fairing the body", a process to be described further on; they have also other uses, which will be referred to in their proper place.

Preparing the Sheer Draft

The portion of the design which contains the three plans we have just been describing, together with the positions of decks, ports, and general out-

line of the hull, is termed the sheer draft, and this is the drawing which is chiefly required in laying off. Other data are required, but these will be given in their proper places; at present we will confine our attention to the sheer draft. And here it may be remarked that the several processes of laying off are dealt with in the following pages in the same order as the draftsman lays off his ship upon the mold-loft floor.

Before proceeding further, it is necessary that we should examine the sheer draft in order that we may become acquainted and familiarize ourselves with the names and uses of the various lines composing it.

Fig. 4 shows the sheer draft of a sloop of war. This is a fair type of a sheer draft as prepared at the Admiralty for the construction of vessels in dockyards. In Fig. 4, the lines marked 2WL, 3WL, etc., are the projections of the intersections with the surface of the ship of planes parallel to the load water plane; they with LWL, the intersection of the load water plane, are called water lines. It may be here remarked that, unless it is otherwise stated, by "the surface of a ship" is meant the outside of the frames and not of the exterior plank, as, after the form of the ship has been designed, the plank is taken off by a process to be afterward described, and thus the building draft shows the surface of the frames.

The dotted perpendicular lines at the extremities, marked FP and AP, are the perpendiculars between which the length of the ship is measured. The other perpendicular lines in the sheer and half-breadth are termed square stations; they are projections, upon these plans, of intersections of transverse vertical planes with the ship's surface. In the body plan is projected only the intersections of the planes with the port side of that portion of the ship on the foreside of her fullest part or dead flat. By this means we have, without confusion, the projections in the body plan of the whole of the traces of these vertical planes with the surface. At the present time the alphabetical designations are sometimes discontinued, and the numerical mode is used for the two bodies, commencing forward or aft, as the case may be. These plane sections are made at the joints of the two sets of timbers composing wooden frames, and at the sides of angle iron frames; they are generally equidistant. Until within recent years it was customary to make the dead flat interval five-fourths the breadth of the others, this being done in order to allow room for a single timber frame, about which the relative positions of the component timbers of the frames

were shifted, all the timbers on the fore side of the single timber being disposed by a certain rule, and those abaft it being disposed in a contrary manner. It should be further stated that the spaces between the joints of the frames of some recently constructed wooden war ships have been greater towards the extremities than at amidships, in order to lighten the framing at those parts which receive least buoyant support.

Again, referring to Fig. 4, TS is the topside line, and besides this the form of the upper deck, as projected in the three plans, is also shown; these are given in order to represent the form of the vessel above the water lines. Generally, a line, termed a top-breadth line, is drawn somewhere between the topside and load water line; and, in large ships, lines at the port sills are given for the same purpose.

The lines marked K show the upper and lower edges of the keelson, and at their extremities are shown the stemson and sternson.

The dotted line marked A is the upper part of the keel, the two lines next below are the upper and lower edges of rabbet of keel; and below these are shown, in succession, the lower edge of keel and the two pieces of false keel. The lines marked UDL in the sheer plan are, beginning at the uppermost, the lines of upper side of upper deck at middle line, upper side of upper deck beams at middle line, and upper side of upper deck beams at the ship's side respectively; these being usually known as deck at middle, beam at middle, and beam at side lines. The vertical distance between the first and second is, of course, the thickness of deck plank; that between the second and third is the round up of the beam. It is at once seen that the latter meet at the extremities of the deck. Besides the lines just noticed, there are also shown the knee of head, head rails, stern and munions, ports, masts and other details.

The upper edge of rabbet of keel is selected as the base line of the sheer draft shown in Fig. 4. This is a conventional usage which is adopted when, as in the present instance, the joints of the frames are perpendicular to the keel. Before passing on, it should be stated that the line termed the upper edge of rabbet, which is usually chosen as a base line, is incorrectly named, being merely a line parallel to the lower edge of rabbet—a fixed line— and distant from it the thickness of the bottom plank. By making this the base line, and the ship not being on an even keel, causes the water lines to be curved in the body plan, as shown. In many cases the frames stand perpendicular to the LWL, and in such

cases a line drawn parallel to the latter, and near the keel, has been chosen as a base, thus causing the square stations in the body plan to end successively one below the other, as shown by Fig. 5 in the next chapter, instead of mostly at a point, as in Fig. 4, and the water lines in such drawings are known as level lines.

Fairing the Ship

The sheer draft is usually prepared on a scale of ¼-inch to a foot. This is copied full size upon the mold loft floor, in performing which operation it is found that errors, almost inappreciable in the one-quarter scale drawing, become very apparent when thus magnified 48 times. The three plans which, when upon paper, coincide as nearly as the draftsman's powers will permit, when copied to full size are found to disagree sufficiently to prevent the various problems of laying off from being solved with that degree of accuracy which is necessary in order to obtain a fair surface to the ship. Hence a fairing, or correcting process, has to be performed before the timbers can be laid off.

The mutual dependence of the three plans upon each other has already been shown; this property is utilized in performing a tentative process, termed fairing the body. It has been shown that the projections of each of the sets of lines generally used in this process, viz., level lines, square stations, bow lines, and diagonal lines, appear straight in one or two of the plans; so that, by the aid of a straight-edged batten, they can be drawn fair very readily in such plans. The property which a wooden or metallic batten has of bending in a fair curve, is brought to our aid in drawing the lines fairly in the plans where they appear curved. For, since the intersections of lines with each other are points, the points of intersection of two sets of lines in one plan are transferred to their relative positions in others, so that points which, when in one plan, were in a straight line, are now in a curved line; a batten is penned, or bent to pass through as many of the points as is consistent with absolute fairness, and the line is drawn. Thus, by a series of interchanges, the various lines are copied from one plan into another, until at length all the plans coincide, the lines composing them are continuous curves; and, having thus evidence of a continuous surface, the body is said to be fair. We will now go through these operations in detail, commencing by copying the drawing upon the floor.

It is a great advantage if the seams of the boards forming the floor of a mold loft are perfectly straight and parallel, as they thus afford considerable

assistance in the several processes of squaring and drawing parallel lines which are involved in the practice of laying off.

The first thing to be done is to strike a base line on the floor; if the board edges are arranged as just stated, it will be necessary to place the base line either parallel or perpendicular to the lines of the seams. Should the floor be rectangular, about two feet from the wall or other boundary of the floor is a very convenient position for a base line. As before stated, a line parallel to the lower edge of rabbet is usually taken as the base, except in the case already cited. Whichever line, however, is chosen, the depth of the keel, the lower edge of rabbet, and the upper side of keel, are set off from it, at distances measured from the sheer draft; also, the fore and after edges of stem, together with the fore edge of rabbet of stem, which latter is, of course, a continuation of the lower edge of rabbet of keel. The post is next copied with the after edge of its rabbet, also the margin of stern and the various square stations in the sheer plan, including the fore and after perpendiculars. These, with the beam at middle lines, are termed the fixed lines of the sheer plan, being indeed unalterable, except insofar as drawing them fair is concerned. To economize space, the half-breadth plan is generally drawn upon the same part of the floor as the sheer plan, the base line of the former, or a line parallel thereto, serving as the middle line of the latter, and in this way the same square stations will do for the two plans. There are few mold-loft floors upon which vessels of more than 100 feet long can be drawn in one length to full size; hence it is necessary to lay them off in two, three, and, in some cases, even more parts. The usual practice, with a wooden ship, is to set off the two perpendiculars at such distances from the ends of the floor, as will permit of the head rails and stern timbers being laid off; whereas with an iron ship, the perpendiculars can be so placed as to just give room for drawing the contour of the stem and the rake of the counter.

When the positions of the perpendiculars are fixed, as much of the fore and after bodies are drawn as the length of the floor will allow, and if there still remains an amidship part, it is laid off separately; so that there are two, or even three, sets of lines overlapping each other. However, since these bodies are not both laid off simultaneously, no confusion occurs.

We will presume that there is room upon our floor to lay off our ship in two parts, and will consider first the fore body, i. e., that portion of the ship on the fore side of dead flat.

To Copy the Body Plan

Having already copied the sheer plan, we will now copy the body plan, doing so as near as possible to the former, at the same time not allowing the lines to cross if it can be avoided. However, this is a mere question of room and convenience. On a small floor the same base line may well serve for the three plans, one of the square stations at amidships being taken as the middle line of the body plan.

A base and middle line for the body plan having been drawn upon the floor, before copying that plan it will be necessary to put certain additional lines in the body plan of the sheet draft, in order to assist the draftsman in copying, and subsequently fairing it. By reference to the sheer draft shown in Fig. 4, it will be seen that the water lines are curved on the body plan. Now the process of fairing is materially assisted if lines which are curved in one plan are straight in another. We have already explained the cause of the curvature of these water lines when projected upon the body plane; we will now draw a series of lines parallel to the base line of the sheer plan, and equidistant from each other. These lines, being produced by the intersections of the surface with planes parallel to the horizontal or half-breadth plane, will appear straight in the body plan, and will, in fact, be drawn similarly to those in the sheer plan. We will therefore draw in the body and sheer plans about as many of those level lines as there were water lines, and copy the lines upon the floor; besides which we will put in level lines near the top side line, top breadth line, and at other intermediate positions, ac-

cording to the height of the ship above the load water line.

Besides these, in order to obtain more numerous and better intersections, a number of diagonal lines are drawn in the body plan. The positions of these lines will be given hereafter; suffice it to say, for the present, that they are the lines of the heads and heels of the timbers, and therefore of the harpins and sirmarks.

Having transferred these lines to the floor, we proceed to copy the body plan by measuring, with a scale, the distances, along the several level and diagonal lines, from the middle line to where they cut the square stations, and then setting off these distances to full size on the corresponding lines upon the floor. Battens are then penned or bent, so as to approximate as closely to these points as is consistent with absolute fairness or continuity, and the lines are marked in with thin slices of chalk.

Table of Ordinates

At some yards it is customary to measure these ordinates, etc., and record them upon paper in a tabulated form before proceeding to draw the body to full size on the floor; and thus the latter operation is performed without direct reference to the drawing when working on the floor. The square stations thus drawn upon the floor are ended as follows: The lines of the half sidings of keel, stem, and sternpost, are drawn in the body and half-breadth plans from dimensions furnished by the specifications or scheme of scantlings, which also states the taper, if any, which these parts of the ship should have. Next, the distance from the base line of sheer at which each square station cuts the lower or fore edge of rabbet, is set off from the base line of body upon the middle line of that plan, and from this point a line is squared out to the half siding of keel, stem, or sternpost. A circle is then swept with the point thus obtained as a center, and a radius equal to the thickness of the bottom plank, and the square station is ended as a tangent to this circle upon the side of the latter, which is nearest to the middle line of body. It should be noticed that this ending is approximate.

CHAPTER II

Fairing the Lines

THE half-breadth plan has next to be drawn upon the floor; and here we may again note that lines now being used, which are curved in the body plan, will be straight in the half-breadth plan, and vice versa. Before proceeding to copy the half-breadth plan from the body plan, it should be noticed that, owing to the new level lines which have been penciled on the sheer drawing, the half-breadth plan to be drawn upon the floor will be totally dissimilar in appearance to that given in the design. But if the base line of the sheer draft is parallel to the water lines, and the body is therefore given in that drawing as shown in Fig. 5, the additional work of copying the body by new lines, and then transferring the latter to the half-breadth plan, will be unnecessary.

Having already drawn on the floor the middle line of the half-breadth plan, and the projections of the square stations in that plan we proceed to copy the level lines from the body into the half-breadth plan (see Fig. 6).

Straight-edged battens are set to the middle lines of body and half-breadth. Then measure on a staff, whose end is kept against the former batten, the distance from the middle line to where a level line ab cuts each square station 1, 2, 3, etc., in the body plan, and transfer these distances to the corresponding square stations in the half-breadth plan, by setting the end of the staff against the middle line batten of that plan, and marking the distances out on the respective square stations. A batten is then bent so as to pass fairly through as many as possible of these points, and the line a_2b_2 is chalked in, this process being performed for each level line.

Still referring to Fig. 6, square down from the sheer plan to the middle line of the half-breadth plan, the point of intersection a_1 of the level line with the fore edge of rabbet of stem, and set off on this perpendicular line the half siding of stem at this height as measured from the body plan. Then end the level line by making it a tangent to a circle whose center is the point thus found, and whose radius is equal to the thickness of the bottom plank, taking care to do so on that side of the circle nearest to the middle line of body. We must again remark that this ending is only approximate unless the stem is square to the level line. For the fore edge of the rabbet is assumed to be the axis of a curved cylinder, the radius of which is the thickness of the bottom plank; and the surface of the timbers is supposed to be in contact with this cylinder along the line of the center of rabbet. It is evident, then, that unless the section of the cylinder is made square to the axis it will be elliptical. Another error is, however, introduced owing to the tapered siding of the stem below the lower cheek.

A more correct ending is, therefore, obtained by making the level line end as a tangent to an ellipse of great or less eccentricity in proportion as the stem deviates much or little from the condition mentioned. However, practically, these endings are sufficiently correct, being within the limits of error to which work is carried out upon the mold-loft floor.

The Bearding Line

It is necessary at this stage of the work to get in the bearding line, i. e., the true line of the after edge of rabbet of stem or upper edge of rabbet of keel, that given in the sheer draft being not sufficiently correct to be copied from thence to the floor. The bearding line is the line of the intersection of the surface of keel, deadwood, stem, and stern post, with the outer surface of the frame timbers; hence a rough, and, indeed, a common way of finding this line, is by measuring in the body plan the half siding of stem at each level line, and drawing, in the half-breadth plan, a line parallel to the middle line of that plan at a distance equal to the half siding thus found. The intersection of this parallel line with the corresponding level line in the half-breadth plan will be, approximately, a point in the bearding line; and if this point be squared into the sheer plan to the corresponding level line, we shall have an approximation to a point in the bearding line in that plan. Other points in the bearding line below the level lines in the sheer are obtained by measuring in the half-breadth plan, the half siding of keel at each square station, and drawing a line in the body parallel to the middle line of that plan, and distant from it the half siding thus found; the intersection of this parallel line with the corresponding square station, when transferred to the respective square station in the sheer plan, will be an approximation to a point in the bearding line in that plan. There is an error in this method of obtaining the bearding line due to the same causes as the incorrectness of the endings of the level lines already referred to. However, it is usually sufficiently correct for all practical purposes, and if slight allowances be made in ending the lines by substituting ellipses for circles according to the discretion of the draftsman, no error worthy of notice will occur.

More Correct Mode of Drawing the Bearding Line

At some yards it is usual to obtain the bearding line and middle of rabbet by the following method, which is obviously more accurate than the preceding, although even this is not theoretically correct, as the taper of the stem is not taken into account. At any selected points A and C on the fore edge of stem, Fig. 7, in the sheer plan, about the same distance from each other as the level lines, draw lines AB and CD perpendicular to the stem; these will be the vertical traces of planes which are perpendicular to the stem and to the sheer plane. Where either of these lines, say CD, cuts the square stations 1, 2, 3, etc., draw lines EG, FH, and DK perpendicular to CD. Then measure the heights of these intersections E, F and D above the base line of sheer, and set them up

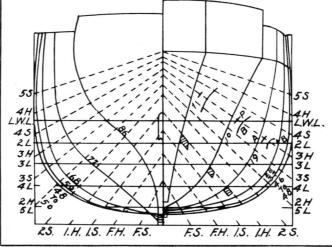

FIG. 5—WATERLINES AND DIAGONALS

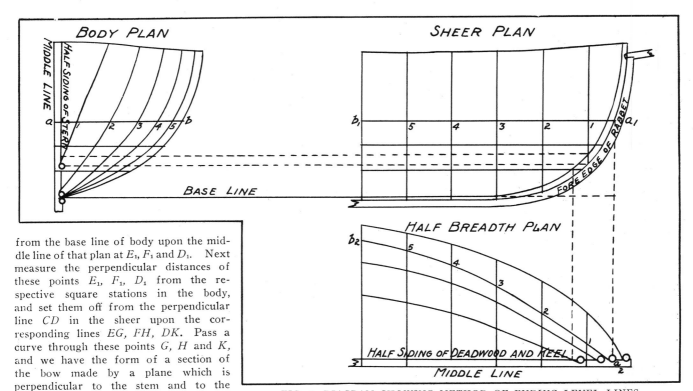

FIG. 6—DIAGRAM SHOWING METHOD OF ENDING LEVEL LINES

from the base line of body upon the middle line of that plan at E_1, F_1 and D_1. Next measure the perpendicular distances of these points E_1, F_1, D_1 from the respective square stations in the body, and set them off from the perpendicular line CD in the sheer upon the corresponding lines EG, FH, DK. Pass a curve through these points G, H and K, and we have the form of a section of the bow made by a plane which is perpendicular to the stem and to the sheer plane, the section being rabatted upon this latter plane.

To end this section, measure the height of the point L (where the line CD cuts the fore edge of rabbet) above the base line of the sheer plan, and set it up on the middle line of body, measuring from the base line of that plan. Then take the half siding of stem at that height, and set it out from the point L perpendicular to CD; with the point S, so found, as center, and with a radius equal to the thickness of the bottom plank, sweep a circle, and end the curve KHG as a tangent to this circle upon the side of it nearest to CD. A line SM drawn through the center S of the circle parallel to CD, will intersect the curve

$KHGT$ in a point M, from which a line MP perpendicular to CD will determine a point P on the latter which will be a point in the bearding line. A perpendicular TO from the point of contact T of the curve with the circle upon the line CD, will give a point O in the middle of rabbet. By following a similar course with the other perpendicular lines AB, etc., points are obtained by which the bearding line and middle of rabbet may be drawn. Both body and half-breadth plans are now upon the floor, the latter having been obtained from the former.

In drawing the lines of the half-breadth plan, it will be found that they

do not pass through all the points determined for them from the body plan, hence, as yet, these plans do not quite agree with each other. We may now proceed to correct the body plan from the half-breadth plan by reversing the preceding process, and thus draw new square stations in the former plan, having previously rubbed out those originally drawn.

Further Test of Fairness

But it is found advisable, before doing this, to institute a greater check upon the square stations in the body plan, than can be made with level lines only. This is done by projecting and

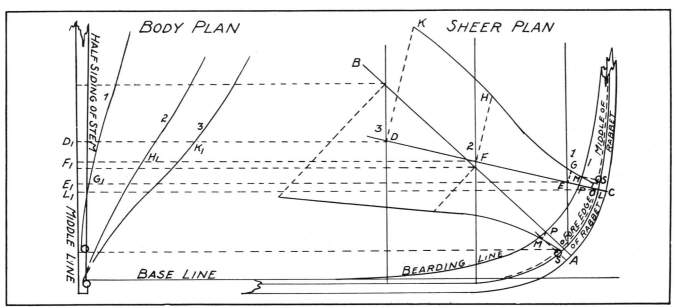

FIG. 7—CORRECT METHOD OF DRAWING BEARING LINE

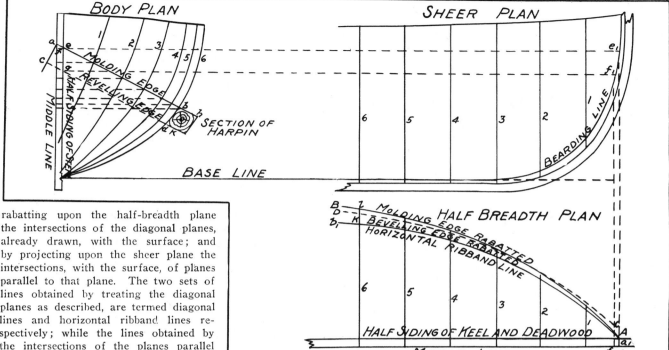

FIG. 8—DIAGRAM SHOWING METHOD OF DRAWING A HORIZONTAL RIBBAND LINE

rabatting upon the half-breadth plane the intersections of the diagonal planes, already drawn, with the surface; and by projecting upon the sheer plane the intersections, with the surface, of planes parallel to that plane. The two sets of lines obtained by treating the diagonal planes as described, are termed diagonal lines and horizontal ribband lines respectively; while the lines obtained by the intersections of the planes parallel to the sheer plane, are known as bow lines when in the fore body, and buttock lines when in the after body.

The diagonal lines and horizontal ribband lines are valuable as checks upon the fairness of the ship, inasmuch as, being in planes which are nearly perpendicular to her surface, they give more determinate intersections; besides which, they afford an excellent criterion of the nature of that surface.

The bow and buttock lines are valuable only at the extremities of the ship; and, there, more as a criterion by which the experienced draftsman can decide whether or not the character of the surface is such as it should be, than as a means of fairing the body, owing to

the general indeterminateness of their intersections.

Hence, some draftsmen test the fore and after ends of the ship by bow and buttock lines, before proceeding to fair the body; as it sometimes happens when the body has been carefully faired by level lines, by "running in" a few bow and buttock lines, a radical defect in the character of the surface is discovered, which necessitates a repetition of the whole fairing process.

Before proceeding to fair the body by means of the diagonals, or lines of

heads and heels of timbers, it must be remarked, that as neither of the planes of projection is parallel to the diagonal plane, in order to obtain the true form of intersection of the diagonal plane must be rabatted upon either the half-breadth or sheer planes. The former is that generally chosen, and, as before stated, the line so obtained is termed a diagonal line.

To Draw a Horizontal Ribband Line

Measure the distance, Fig. 8, square to the middle line of the body plan at which a diagonal line *ab* cuts each

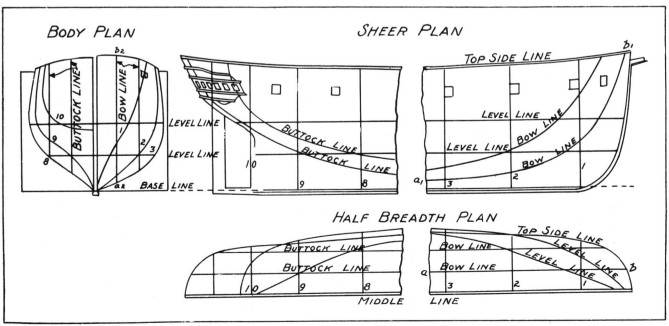

FIG. 9—BUTTOCK LINES AND BOW LINES

square station 1, 2, 3, etc., and set off these distances from the middle line of the half-breadth plan upon the corresponding square stations. A line a_1b_1 drawn through these points is the horizontal ribband line.

Measure the perpendicular distance from the base line of body, to where the diagonal ab cuts the half siding of stem, and set that distance up square to the base line of the sheer plan, to where it intersects the bearding line at e_1, from which point square a line e_1e_2 to the middle line of half-breadth, and measure from the base line upon the line e_2e_1, a distance e_2a_1 equal to half siding of stem ef at the height of the point e. The point a_1, thus found is the ending of the horizontal ribband line.

In fairing the bodies of wall-sided ships, the horizontal ribband lines frequently

ribband line—a point A is thus determined at which the diagonal is to be ended.

Bow and Buttock Lines

We will now turn our attention to the bow and buttock lines. Since the sheer and half-breadth plans overlap each other on the floor, and have the base and middle line of these plans, respectively, coincident; as a matter of convenience, the level lines in the former plan may be used as bow and buttock lines for the latter. In the body plan, these lines will be drawn parallel to the middle line, and at the same distance from it as they are from the middle line of the half-breadth plan. The bow and buttock lines are drawn only as far from the extremities toward amidships, as curvature of a peculiar character may extend.

Where the bow line ab, Fig. 9, in

the bow line as the batten will spring to. As we have already stated bow and buttock lines are of great service to both designer and draftsman in judging the character of the surface at the extremities of the ship. No rules can be laid down for guidance in dealing with them, experience being required in order that they may afford a vivid conception of the form of the vessel.

The body plan may now be recopied, and the new square stations drawn in and ended as before. If these do not pass through all the points obtained for them, the half-breadth plan must again be checked by it, and so on, alternately, these operations must be repeated until the body and half-breadth plans exactly coincide, and both plans have fair or continuous lines in them.

In practically performing these

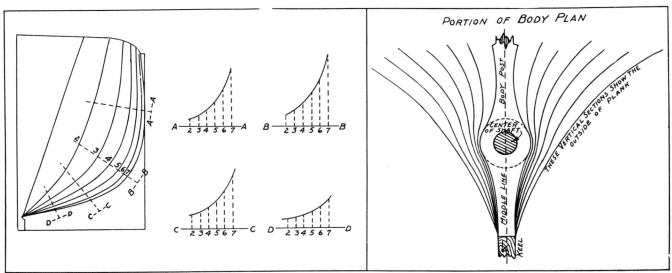

FIG. 10—CONTRACTED METHOD OF FAIRING.   FIG. 11— ACCOUNTING FOR SWELL FOR SCREW SHAFT

quently coincide, or are so near each other as to be indistinguishable. In such a case it is advisable to use the rabatted instead of the projected intersection of the diagonal plane, i.e., to fair by diagonals. Indeed, in any case it is advantageous to draw these lines in fairing, as they must be laid off at some time or another in order that the molds may be made for the harpins.

In Fig. 8, measure along the direction of the diagonal line ab in the body plan, the distance from the middle line of that plan to where the diagonal cuts each square station, 1, 2, etc., and set off these distances in the half-breadth plan upon the corresponding square stations, measuring from the middle line. A curve AB passed through these points is the diagonal required.

To end the diagonal line, measure the half siding of stem ae in the body plan along the direction of the diagonal line, and set up this distance on the perpendicular line e_2e_1 already drawn through the ending of the horizontal

the halfbreadth plan intersects with each level line, square up to the corresponding level line in the sheer plan, and the points thus determined are in the bow line. Next, take the heights above the base line of the body plan, at which the bow line cuts each square station, and set up these heights in the sheer plan upon the corresponding square stations, measuring from the base line; the points thus obtained will also be in the bow line. Generally, a curve will not pass through all these points, owing to the indeterminateness of the intersections at some parts, as well as to an unfairness of the surface. Hence, bow and buttock lines require more judgment and discretion in their treatment than either of the other lines by which the body is faired. When discrepancies occur, the level and diagonal lines in the neighborhood must be examined to see if the points of intersection were correctly taken, and if a modification of these lines, consistent with fairness, will give such points for

operations, a great deal must be left to the judgment of the draftsman; a practical eye will save much labor When a batten does not spring well to the points, it is best to pass it outside some and inside others, and thus prevent great deviation from the design in either direction; observing that, as a rule, the batten should pass on the outside more frequently than on the inside of the points, in order that the volume of the ship may not be less than that given by the design. In copying and drawing the body plan, it is advisable to draw the midship section first, and then the others in rotation, as the draftsman is thus better enabled to see what he is doing, and exercise his judgment.

Fairing the After Body

Should the preceding operations have been carefully carried out, the fore body will be fair, and work, which will be treated of subsequently,

can be proceeded with at once. Before entering upon this, we will, however, first consider the after body. All that has been said of the fore body is true of this; a slight variation is, however, made with reference to the bearding lines. Owing to the swell allowed to house the screw shaft, and the general fineness of the after body, which would cause the heels of the timbers to run off to a thin wedge, a somewhat irregular stepping line is cut in the stern post and dead-wood for the endings of the timbers (See Fig. 4). Greater care is required in getting in buttock than bow lines, as owing to the great curvature at the counter, which is in a direction perpendicular to the buttock planes, the intersections are more trustworthy than by any other plans, and, hence, they are almost the only criterion of the fairness at that part. It is well, in fairing the body, to scarf or overlap the lines in the half-breadth plan, that is, to fair a few feet of the midship portion of the ship in both bodies. Perhaps, however, the best way to ensure the ship being fair when the fore and after bodies are joined amidships, is to set off in the half-breadth plan lines parallel to the middle line of that plan, and distant from it the greatest breadths at the several level lines; and take care, when penning the battens to the respective lines, to prevent them from extending beyond the parallel lines.

A Contracted Method of Fairing

The body being fair, we might now proceed to lay off the cants, etc., by it; but, before doing so, we will first show how to fair the body by what is known as the contracted method.

The extremities of a ship are the parts which require the most care in fairing, this being due, not only to the greater curvature at those parts, but also to the fact that most of the problems in laying off occur at the bow and stern.

As we shall see further on, the midship portion of the ship, although by far the largest, is yet that most easily disposed of by the draftsman, and owing to its being so straight, very little fairing is required for it.

To save time and labor, as well as for the advantage derived from being able to do in a small space that which would otherwise occupy a large part of the floor, the body is often faired by the contracted method shown in Fig. 10.

First determine by an examination of the body plan how much of it shall be faired by this method, observing that it is well to leave such portions of the two bodies as may have great curvature to be faired by the method already given. It must be observed, that in the figure, more than the usual portion of the body is shown as being faired by this method.

Draw upon the floor, perpendicular to any chosen base line, as many equidistant straight lines as there are sections to be faired, and number these perpendiculars to represent the square stations. These lines need not be spaced more than a sixth or a seventh of the spacing of the stations apart. Next, produce each level and diagonal line (diagonal line usually) in the body plan to any point chosen at a few feet beyond the midship section, the reason for this will be seen presently. Then measure along each level and diagonal line from the termination outside the body plan just fixed upon, to where is intersects with each of the square stations to be faired; set these distances upon the corresponding perpendicular lines just drawn, measuring, of course, from the base line; and draw lines, by a batten, through these points. Treat all the level and diagonal lines in a similar manner; and at the top sides use level lines drawn in the same places as when fairing that part of the ship by the ordinary method. Fair these lines in the same manner as if the spacing of the perpendiculars were the correct room and space. Alternate the processes by recopying the body from these curved lines, and vice versa, until the curves pass fairly through all the points obtained for them, after which this fictitious half-breadth plan may be rubbed out, the midship portion of the body being faired. Assume the two endmost of the stations so faired to be absolute and invariable; and in fairing the extremities of the ship by the ordinary method, let the batten pass through all the spots in these stations in the same manner as if it mere the midship section, taking care, however, to let the batten pass through points obtained from the adjacent stations, so that there may be no discontinuity in the surface of the ship where the portion of the body faired by the contracted method joins to that faired by the ordinary method.

One of the chief advantages of the method of fairing which we have just been describing, consists in the facility with which the molds of the square body can be sent out, and the timbers converted before the fairing of the extremities of the ship is completed.

It may be remarked, that when the square stations are not equidistant, it will be necessary to space the perpendicular lines, by which the curves are set off, at distances from each other proportional to the spacing of the square stations. There is no necessity for using the level and diagonal lines already in the body, as any lines may be used for the purpose of fairing.

It will be readily seen that not only is the contracted method correct in principle, but owing to the ordinates of the curve being placed closer together, the curvature is increased, and, therefore, the battens are more likely to spring fairly than when the curves are nearly straight.

Projections of Diagonals on the Sheer Plan

We will now get in a set of lines, which, although seldom used for the purpose of fairing, yet serve to prove that fairness, when drawing upon paper. The lines referred to are the projections of the diagonal lines on the sheer plane. The chief use of these lines is to give the positions of the heads and heels of the timbers when disposed in the sheer plan, upon boards which are given to the workmen for their guidance in fairing the ship.

It has been already remarked, that diagonals are used as harpin lines; of these diagonals there are two sets, viz., heads or harpins, and filling heads or sirmarks. The former give the lines of the heads of frame timbers, and the latter of filling or doubling frames. An arrangement of diagonals in the body plan is shown by Fig. 5; those marked FH, 1H, 2H, etc., being the floor head, first head, second head, etc., harpins, respectively; while those marked I-S, 1st S, 2nd S, etc., are the floor sirmark, first sirmark, second sirmark, etc., respectively. The same names are given to the corresponding diagonals in the half-breadth and sheer plans. At some yards a different nomenclature is adopted; the sirmarks FS, 1st S, 2nd S, etc., being known as S.F.H., F.F.H., F. 1st H, etc., or short floor head, filling floor head, filling first head, etc., while the same names, as before stated, are given to the heads of the frame timbers.

The diagonals in the sheer plan are generally copied upon paper to a ¼-inch scale, being laid off from the sheer draft without reference to the floor. When the frames are disposed, the drawing is copied upon a board and given to the workmen for their guidance, as before stated.

Measure the height, Fig. 12, square from the base line of the body plan, at which a diagonal line ab cuts each square station, 1, 2, 3, etc., and set these distances upon the corresponding

square stations in the sheer, measuring from the base line of that plan. A line $a_1 b_1$, drawn through these points is the diagonal in the sheer plan. Diagonal lines are generally ended at the bearding line, and the ending is obtained by measuring the height above the base line of the body plant at which the diagonal cuts the half siding of stem or stern post and setting this height square from the base line in the sheer to cut the bearding line; the point on the bearding line, so obtained, is the ending of the diagonal.

Intermediate Sections

Up to the present time we have been working with only every second, third, or perhaps fourth square station drawn in each plan. These were

the plans. Measure with a scale from the sheer draft the height above the base line of the sheer plan at which the top side, top-breadth, or other such line, cuts each square station and set up these heights on the corresponding square station in the sheer, and pass a batten through as many of the points, so found, as is consistent with fairness. It will be found, that this line will not differ materially from a line copied upon the floor previous to the body being faired. When the line is copied into the sheer plan, it can be transferred to the body plan, by measuring the height above the base line at which it intersects each square station, and setting up these heights upon the corresponding square stations in the

It should be remarked that the scantling taken for the radius does not usually include the boxen wood allowed in lieu of the bottom planking. The after square stations are then bent, so that all which would otherwise intersect with this circle are made tangents to it. The bent portions of these square stations are then faired by putting additional level lines in the vicinity of the swell, transferring them to the half-breadth plan, and recopying the stations as before described. After this is done, the lines of the outside of the plank are drawn parallel to these, and the molds to the stern post, etc., are made to the outer lines, thus allowing for the boxen. Fig. 11 shows the outer lines.

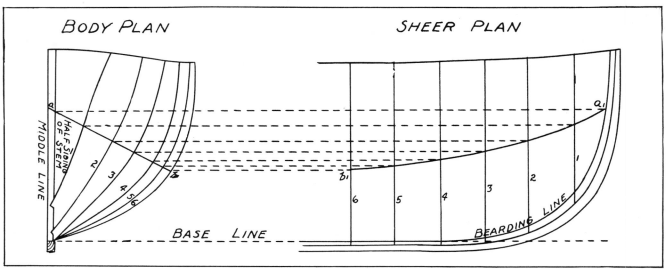

FIG. 12—DIAGRAM SHOWING METHOD OF DRAWING DIAGONALS IN SHEER PLAN

sufficient to fair the body by; and, indeed, were preferable to having the whole of these stations drawn, owing to the greater clearness resulting from fewer lines being drawn upon the floor.

The intermediate stations may now be supplied. As these stations appear straight in the sheer and half-breadth, they are first drawn in those plans by dividing the space between two consecutive square stations, as at present drawn, into the requisite number of equal parts, and drawing vertical lines through the points thus obtained. They are then easily transferred from these plans into the body plan by the methods already given. If the body is fair, the new square stations will pass through all the points set off for them.

Either at this stage of the work, or before putting in the intermediate square stations, it is necessary to draw the top side line, top-breadth line, and other lines which at all conform to the sheer of the ship. These lines will appear curved in all

body plan, measuring square from the base line of that plan. A curve passed through the points so obtained, will be the projection in the body plan of the sheer line referred to. To transfer the line to the half-breadth plan, measure the distance square from the middle line of the body plan at which the sheer line cuts each square station, and set these distances upon the corresponding square stations in the half-breadth, measuring from the middle line of that plan. A curve passed through these points will be the horizontal projection of the sheer line. The sheer lines are ended at the bearding line similarly to the horizontal ribband lines.

When the after body of a screw ship has been faired, the height and directions of the center of screw shaft are drawn in the body and sheer plans. A circle is then swept in the former plan, the center of which is the center of shaft, and the radius is that of the shaft plus the scantling of timber which is allowed around it.

The square stations in the body plan have been ended as tangents to circles, each having a radius equal to the thickness of the bottom planks. If the center of a circle be joined to the point where the square station touches it, and the side of the keel be drawn, we shall have the shape of the rabbet of keel at the section in question, on the supposition that the garboard strakes are the same thickness as the bottom plank. Sometimes thick garboards or Lang's safety keels are fitted. The floors are scored down $1\frac{1}{2}$ inches into the keel, $\frac{3}{4}$ inch being taken out of each; and the under side of the floor is snaped away in a straight line to a point termed the angle of floor. This point is given in the midship section; and, in order that the edge of the outer piece of garboard may be a fair curve, and parallel to the general run of the bottom planking at that part, the draftsman measures with his compasses the distance between the center of rabbet and the angle

of floor in the midship section; and with the former point as a center, sweeps a circular arc in the body plan to cut the square stations at points, each of which will be the angle of floor for that section. The shape of the floor for each section is then obtained, by joining a point 1½ inches below the upper part of keel with the angle of floor at that section. It will be observed that, as the stations get more perpendicular forward and aft, the lines of the underside of floors, as thus drawn merge into the curves of the frames until the angle disappears. Sometimes only the square body frames have been treated in this way; the timbers of what is termed the cant body, which we shall consider in a future chapter, being made to heel against the bearding line. Hence, below the angle of floor, these timbers have projected beyond those of the square body. Of course, this has only been the case when the cant body has commenced nearer amidships, than where the angle of floor has merged into the curvature of the frames. A fair surface has been given to the ship's bottom in such a case, either by scoring the garboard plank over this projection, or by putting the garboards in two thicknesses, the inner of which has flushed the surface before the outer was put on.

The cutting down line is the line of the upper side of the floors at the middle line in the square body, and of the upper side of the heels of the timbers in the cant body. It should now be drawn.

The position of this line is governed by the shape of the body and the molding of the timbers. It is usually obtained by setting in square to the surface at each square station in the body plan, the molding of the timber at its ending, to where that distance cuts the half siding of either stem deadwood or stern post, according to the situation of the ending. Such a point will be the height of cutting down at that square station, that is, the minimum height to which the deadwood need come in order to completely house the heel of the timber in the cant body; it is also the top of the floors, at middle line, in the square body. Points such as these are obtained for each square station in the body plan, then these heights are transferred to the corresponding stations in the sheer plan; and a line drawn through the points so obtained gives the cutting down line.

We have just stated that the moldings of the timbers are set in square to the surface of the ship. Now, at amidships, it will be sufficient if we merely set the molding of the timber in a direction square to the curve of the station; but at the extremities, especially in a bluff ship, it is evident that the distance thus set in would be considerably less than the actual thickness of the timber; we have therefore to obtain the accurate molding of the timber in the plane of the square station, before we can draw in a correct cutting down line at the extremities. Such moldings, from a practical point of view, are difficult to obtain perfectly accurate.

Just as the bearding line is the line of the endings of the outer sides of the timbers, so the cutting down line is that of their inner sides. They are, in fact, respectively, the traces of the planes of the side of stem, stern post, and deadwood with the outer and inner surfaces of the frame timbers. In proportion, then, as the ship is full or sharp at her extremities, so will these lines be near to each other or far apart. Now, as a sufficient molded width of stem, apron, stern post, deadwood, etc., is required to provide heeling and security to the cant frames, it is evident that the cutting down line will regulate the dimensions of the fore and after ends of the backbone of the ship. The deadwood usually projects about 1 inch beyond the cutting down line, but in some instances, when the ships have been very sharp, it has been found necessary to reduce the molded width of the deadwood in order to save weight, by allowing the cutting down line to run along the keelson, and thus partially heeling the cants against the latter; this, however, should be avoided when possible, as the keelson is considerably weakened by receiving the bolts from the heels of the timbers.

Even before we have arrived at this stage of the work, the drawing on the floor is sufficiently advanced for molds to be made for the frames of the square body, and other information to be supplied from it, by means of which the workmen can begin to prepare many of the timbers of the ship.

Index

PAGE

Accidents, Methods of Avoiding, During Vessel Construction 75

After Body, Drawing the, on the Mold-Loft Floor....41, 91

After End of the Ship, Framing of the.............. 54

Air Seasoned Material, Average Strength Values for Structural Timbers 9

Apron, Definition of.........................47, 50

Arch Strapping, Employment of.................... 45

Assembling the Frame Sections.................... 44

Axioms and Definitions........................... 89

Ballin, Fred A., Advanced Form of Construction, Designed by 5

Ballin, Fred A., Design of Steel Strapping Worked Out by 26

Ballin, Fred A., Description of 4000-Ton Motor Ship, Designed by 30

Batten, Use of, in Preparing the Molds............. 41

Battens, Use of, in Trimming the Timbers.......... 51

Beam, Taking the Snape of a...................... 80

Beams, Efficiency of Hold and Main Deck.......... 73

Beams, Marking in the Line of the................ 80

Beams, Rasing in the Line for the................. 79

Beams, Two-Fold Service of, in Deck Construction.. 78

Bearding Line, Drawing in the.................... 92

Bearding of the Rudder Post...................... 83

Beveling Machine, Designed by Stetson Machine Works, Description of........................ 71

Beveling of Rudder Stocks....................... 84

Beveling the Timbers............................. 53

Body Plans, Copying the......................... 91

Body Plan of a Vessel, Copying the, onto the Mold-Loft Floor 43

Bow Construction of Modern Wooden Ships........ 47

Box for Softening Planks......................... 67

British Architect on the Double Diagonal Planking System 30

Building Slips, Preparing the..................... 33

Buildings Necessary for Shipyard.................. 18

Buttock Lines, Importance of..................... 57

Butts, Disposition of, in Planking................. 66

Cant Frames, Securing the, to the Keel and Deadwood 50

Carlings, Definition of........................... 78

PAGE

Carrying Capacity of Wooden Ships of Standard Pacific Coast Type........................... 32

Caulking the Deck................................ 81

Ceiling, Laying the............................... 71

Cost of Equipment and Buildings for Small Shipyard 19

Cranes Used in Shipyard Work.................... 22

Cross Section of Typical Wooden Ship............. 3

Cutting-Down Line, Drawing in the............... 98

Deadwood, Arrangement of the.................... 50

Deadwood, Heeling to the.......................45, 47

Deck Beams, Two Different Forms of Construction... 75

Deck Elements, Construction of................... 75

Deck Finishing, Arranging for the................. 80

Deck Fittings for Wooden Ship.................... 86

Deck Planks, Laying the.......................... 80

Definitions and Axioms.......................... 89

Derricks Used in Shipyard Work.................. 22

Design and Layout of Shipyard................... 18

Design for Typical Wooden Vessel................. 3

Design of a 4000-ton Motor Ship, Built by Supple & Ballin 30

Diagonal System of Planking..................... 32

Diagonals, Projection of, on the Sheer Plan......... 96

Dollies for Use in Shipyard Work................. 22

Douglas Fir, Average Strength Value for........... 9

Drift-Bolts as Fastenings......................... 13

Dubbing-Off the Outer Surface of the Ship......... 66

Edge Bolting as a Means of Fastening Elements Together 13

Elliptical Stern, Construction of................... 61

Engine Foundations in Wooden Ships, Preparation of 85

Engines, Cost of Installing Oil, in Modern Motor Ship 86

Entrance to Vessel During Construction............ 75

Equipment Necessary for Shipyard................ 19

Exit to Vessel During Construction................ 75

Fairing, a Contracted Method of.................. 96

Fairing the Line................................. 92

Fairing the Ship...............................41, 90

Page

Fantail Stern, Construction of........................ 61
Fastening for Planking............................... 67
Fastening Sawed Frame Futtocks Together.......... 44
Fastenings in Ship Construction..................... 13
Fastenings, Use of Metal............................ 67
Ferris, Theodore E., Steel Strapping, as Designed by 26
Fibre Stress for Fir or Pine......................... 10
Fir, Preparing Douglas, for Use..................... 8
Fir, Production of Douglas, in the United States
    in 1915 7
Fir, Typical Properties of Douglas.................. 8
Fore Body, Drawing the, on the Mold-Loft Floor..41, 91
Formula for Estimating Carrying Capacity of
    Wooden Ships 32
Forward End of Ship, Methods of Framing.......... 47
Frame, Assembling the............................... 44
Frame of Modern Wooden Vessel, Specifications of
    Timbers Needed for............................ 43
Frame Timbers, Marking and Sawing the............ 44
Frame, Raising the, into Position................... 44
Framing the After End of the Ship................. 54
Framing the Ship, Time Required for............... 43
Framing the Vessel.................................. 38
Futtocks, Assembling the............................ 44

Geometry, Application of, to Shipbuilding........... 87
Grays Harbor Shipbuilding Co., Description of Stand-
    ard 5-Masted Auxiliary Schooner, Built by...... 29
Great Lakes Type of Wooden Vessel, Description of 26
Green Lumber, Average Strength Value for Structural
    Timbers 9

Half-Breadth Plan, Copying the, on the Mold-Loft
    Floor 43, 91, 92
Hang, Determining the Amount of.................. 70
Hatch Construction in a 4000-ton Wooden Steamer... 30
Hatchways, Formation of the....................... 80
Head Frames, Definition of......................... 47
Heeling to the Deadwood......................45, 47
Hoisting Equipment Necessary in Shipyard.......... 19
Hold Bracing, Construction of...................... 73
Hold for the Frame Sections, Preparing the......... 41
Hold Stanchions, Methods for Framing.............. 73
Horning the Frame................................. 45
Hulls, Weaknesses of Wooden...................... 3
Hull Weights of a Motor Schooner................. 32

Internal Combustion Motors, Advantages of, in Fuel
    Economy 3

Keel Blocks, Laying the............................ 33
Keel, Laying the................................... 38

Page

Keelson Construction in a 4000-ton Wooden Steamer 30
Keelson, Construction of........................... 71
Keelson Construction on a Typical Pacific Coast
    Vessel 29
Kirby, Frank E., Method of Construction, Patented by 5
Knees, Types of.................................... 80
Knightheads, Definition of......................... 47
Knuckle of an Elliptical Stern..................... 61

Labor Necessary on Planking Job................... 67
Labor on the Job, Economy of not Overcrowding... 32
Launching of Wooden Ships........................ 86
Launching Ways, Preparing the, for the Construction
    of the Ship.................................... 33
Laying Off the Ship...........................41, 87
Layout of Shipyard................................ 18
Loblolly Pine, Average Strength Values for.......... 9
Logging Operations on the Pacific Coast............ 8
Long-Leaf Pine, Average Strength Value for........ 9
Lumber Cut in the United States for 1915 by States 10
Lumber, No. 1 Common, Specifications for Standard
    Grade 10
Lumber Production for 1915 in the United States..... 7
Lumber Supply in Canada.......................... 2
Lumber Supply in the United States................ 2
Lumbering Operations on the Pacific Coast.......... 8

Mast Pole, Framing of............................. 80
Masts, Advantages of Using Steel.................. 83
Men Necessary on Planking Job, Number of........ 67
Men on the Job,, Economy of not Overcrowding.... 32
Mold-Loft, Laying Off the Ship on the............. 91
Molding the Curved Shape of the Timbers.......... 52
Motor Ship, Description of a Full-Powered 4000-ton,
    of Standard Pacific Coast Type................. 29
Motor Ship, Description of 4000-ton, Designed by
    Fred A. Ballin................................. 30
Motive Power Necessary for Propulsion............. 3

Oil Engines, Advantages of, in Fuel Economy....... 2
Oil Engines, Cost of Installing, in Modern Motor
    Ships 86
Ordinates, Use of Table of........................ 91

Pacific Coast Type of Wooden Vessel, Description
    of Standard 29
Painting of Wooden Ships......................... 86
Parabolic Stern, Construction of................... 61
Pine, Production of Southern Yellow in the United
    States in 1915................................. 7
Pine, Typical Properties of Southern Yellow........ 7

INDEX

PAGE

Pintles, Placing of the Rudder.................... 83
Planking of the Ship.......................... 64
Planking System, Double Diagonal................ 30
Planks, Putting on the...................... 67
Power for Wooden Ships........................ 2
Preservatives, Application of.................... 8

Quarter-Block in Stern Construction............... 63

Rabatting, Definition of.......................... 89
Rabbet, Determining the Base by the Lower Edge of 91
Rectangular Construction of Wooden Ships, Weaknesses in 3
Reinforcement of Wooden Vessels................. 5
Ribbands for Holding the Frame Together.......... 44
Roughing Out the Timber....................... 44
Routing Material Through Shipyards.............. 18
Rudder and Rudder Post, Raising of the.......... 62
Rudder Stock, Coning of the.................... 83

Saw Outfit for Shipyard Use.................... 22
Scarfing of the Shelf Timers.................... 75
Scarfing Together Section of the Keel............ 38
Schooner, Description of Standard Type Wooden.... 29
Selected Common, Specifications for............. 10
Shaft Logs, Arrangement of.................... 85
Shaping Timbers for Ship Construction........... 13
Sheer-Draft, Preparation of the................. 41
Sheer Plan, Copying the........................ 91
Sheer Plan, Projection of Diagonals on the........ 96
Shelf, Construction of......................... 75
Ship Timbers, Grades and Characteristics of........ 7
Shipyard, Cost of Equipment for Small............ 19
Shipyard, Design and Layout of................. 18
Shipyards, Cost of Building for Small............ 19
Shipyards, Factors Governing Selection of the Site.. 15
Shrinkage of Douglas Fir........................ 8
Siding the Timber............................. 52
Site for Shipyard, Factors Governing the Selection of... 15
Skidding Equipment Necessary in Shipyard......... 19
Slips, Preparing the Building.................... 33
Snape of a Beam, Taking the.................... 80
Sny, Determining the Amount of................. 70
Southern Practice in Framing.................... 44
Spars, Preparation of.......................... 83
Specifications for No. 1 Common and Selected Common 10
Spikes, Use of, as Fastenings.................... 13
Spiling Batten, for Determining Sny and Hang...... 70
Square Stern, Timbering of the.................. 54
Steamer, Cross Section Details of 4000-ton Wooden 29
Steel Reinforcement for Wooden Vessels...........5, 23
Steel Reinforcing on a Typical Pacific Coast Vessel 29

PAGE

Steel Strapping for Wooden Ships................. 26
Stem, Building Up the.......................... 47
Stem, Fastening of the, to the Keel............... 53
Stern, Different Types of....................... 54
Stern Framing, Details of....................... 54
Stern Post, Raising the, into Place............... 62
Stern Tube, Arrangement of.................... 85
Stetson Machine Works, Description of Beveling Machine, Designed by........................ 71
Strake of Planks, Determining the Amount of Sny or Hang in a.................................. 70
Strakes, Arrangement of the Planking in.......... 64
Strapping, Steel, for Wooden Ships.............. 26
Strength Values for Structural Timbers, Average.... 9
Stress, Fibre, for Fir or Pine................... 10
Structural Timbers, Average Strength Values for.... 9
Supple & Ballin, Arrangements for Routing at the Plant of 18

Timber in the United States and Canada, Total Supply of Merchantable 2
Timbers, Trimming the......................... 50
Tools for Shipyard Work....................... 22
Tools Used in Shaping Timbers.................. 13
Transom Stern, Timbering of the................ 54
Treenails and Fastenings for Planking............ 67
Treenails, Use and Efficiency of................. 13
Trimming of Timbers.......................... 50
Types of Wooden Vessels, Details of Different..... 23
Typical Properties of Southern Pine and Douglas Fir 7
Typical Wooden Vessel Stern.................... 3

United States Emergency Fleet Corporation, Description of Vessels Similar to Those Designed for.... 26

Ward, M. R., System of Steel Strapping as Designed by 26
Ways, Preparing the, for the Construction of Wooden Ships 33
Weights of Timber............................. 8
Weights of Various Items in a Wooden Ship....... 32
Western Hemlock, Average Strength Values for..... 9
White, W. A., On the Merit of the Double Diagonal Planking System 30
Wooden Hulls, Weaknesses Inherent in............ 3
Wooden Ships, Description of Three Typical........ 26
Wooden Ships, the Outboard Profiles and Deck Plans of Standard Type of........................ 27
Wooden Vessels, Details of Different Types of...... 23
Woodworking Machinery for Shipyard Use.......... 22

Yard, Cost of Building for Small Ship............. 19
Yard, Cost of Equipment for Small Ship........... 19
Yards, Factors Governing the Selection of the Site of... 15